Good Things to Eat

Lucas Hollweg

Good Things to Eat

Photography by Tara Fisher

Collins

First published in 2011 by Collins

an imprint of
HarperCollins Publishers
77–85 Fulham Palace Road
London W6 8JB

www.harpercollins.co.uk

15 14 13 12 11
9 8 7 6 5 4 3 2 1

Text © Lucas Hollweg, 2011
Photography © Tara Fisher, 2011

Senior commissioning editor: Lizzy Gray
Senior project editor: Helen Hawksfield
Food stylist: Valerie Berry
Prop stylist: Wei Tang
Design: Fivebargate

Lucas Hollweg asserts his moral right to be identified
as the author of this work.

A catalogue record for this book is available from the
British Library.

ISBN: 978-0-00-736407-7

Printed and bound in China by South China Printing

For Lucie

Contents

This is a book about my favourite things to cook and eat – about the food that makes me hungry and happy.

Food enthusiasms are a personal and emotional thing. Mine have been shaped by all the good things I've ever eaten, the places I've eaten them in and the people I've eaten them with. For me, cooking is a way of recapturing the joy of those moments, whether it's the perfect peach in Naples, a crisp schnitzel and potato salad in a German café or a cumin-scented stew in a Moroccan marketplace. And, underpinning it all, there are the sustaining memories of my Somerset childhood and the good things we ate then.

For years, food was a private rather than public passion. I began writing recipes as a sideline when I was working as a journalist. Over time, those recipes became a column in 'The Sunday Times Style' magazine. Now, as then, my starting points are always the same: what do I feel like eating and what's around at the moment? My aim is equally straightforward: to make something that tastes delicious.

The recipes on these pages are unapologetically simple, but I hope that – whatever your mood, whatever the weather – you will always find something to stoke your appetite. There are stews, roasts, soups and risottos to lift the soul on a winter's day, salads that celebrate all that is vital and fresh and puddings that probably aren't as healthy as they might be – which is pretty much the point of a pud, after all. I hope, too, that in all of them you will find something to encourage and inspire, new adventures with flavours and ingredients that you already love.

If you cook from this book and enjoy what you have made, then I have done my job. These are some of my Good Things to Eat. I hope they will become yours, too.

I've always thought there's something rather brazen about berries and cherries. It's all that voluptuous ripeness and come-hither colour. When nature puts on its lipstick, it can be pretty hard to resist.

Most summer fruit is an easy pleasure, sweet enough to eat straight from the bush, punnet or bowl, the notable exceptions being gooseberries and currants, which need cooking to bring out their toothsome charms. But there's one thing that's guaranteed to make any berry taste even better: cream. Pour a thin thread over the top, whip a bowlful into a light cloud, add a blob of mascarpone or even soft cream cheese. Together, they are one of the world's most perfect edible partnerships.

The fruit does, of course, need to be properly ripe and summery. Berries and cherries are really only worth eating in season. An imported January strawberry may look the part, but it is invariably a flavourless and joyless thing. And there's nothing remotely seductive about that.

Vanilla creams
with gooseberries

Blueberry
and almond tart

Strawberries in red
wine with cream
cheese and basil

Strawberry and
lemon curd tart

Autumn mess
with blackberries

Cherrymisu

Kir and
raspberry jellies

Berries
and
cherries

Vanilla creams with gooseberries

Green gooseberries are not a childish thing. Unlike the sweeter berries, they are too mouthpuckeringly sharp to be eaten just as they are, and need heat and sugar to temper their tartness. The reward for that extra effort, however, is a unique and old-fashioned flavour, and a perfect foil for the delectable softness of these vanilla creams.

For 4
3 leaves of gelatine
250ml (9fl oz) whole milk
250ml (9fl oz) double cream
60g (2¼oz) caster sugar
½ vanilla pod

For the gooseberries:
400g (14oz) gooseberries, topped and tailed
50g (1¾oz) caster sugar
6 tbsp undiluted elderflower cordial

Put the gelatine in a bowl of cold water, pushing it under so it's completely submerged, and leave to soak for 5 minutes, until soft and floppy.

Meanwhile, put the milk, cream and 60g (2¼oz) sugar in a small saucepan. Slit the vanilla pod lengthways and scrape out the black seeds from the middle with the tip of a sharp knife. Add the seeds and pod to the liquid in the pan and bring to a simmer over a low heat, stirring to help the sugar dissolve. Remove from the heat.

Squeeze the gelatine in your hands to get rid of the excess water, then stir into the hot cream mixture until it has totally dissolved. Strain carefully through a sieve into four 150ml (5fl oz) moulds; metal dariole moulds are good if you have them. Leave to cool, then cover with clingfilm and place in the fridge to set overnight.

Meanwhile, poach the gooseberries. Put the fruit in a saucepan with the 50g (1¾ oz) sugar and 2 tablespoons water and bring to a bubble. Turn down the heat and simmer gently for 8–10 minutes, or until the fruit has just popped. Leave to cool, then stir in the elderflower cordial and refrigerate.

Turn out the creams by dipping the moulds in hot water for a few seconds, then upending them onto small plates. Serve each one with some of the gooseberries and their juices.

Blueberry and almond tart

A fruit and almond tart is a particular favourite of mine: left to my own devices, I can happily demolish half a large one at a single sitting.

I make them throughout the year in different guises, changing the fruit with the seasons: poached pears or quinces, fresh raspberries or blackberries, cherries, apricots, prunes or plums. The combination of fruit, buttery almond sponge and short pastry is endlessly irresistible.

Makes a 23cm (9in) tart
1 quantity of sweet pastry (page 260)
175g (6oz) unsalted butter
175g (6oz) caster sugar
3 medium eggs
½ tsp natural vanilla extract
175g (6oz) ground almonds
1 tbsp plain flour, plus more for rolling the pastry
200g (7oz) blueberries
icing sugar and crème fraiche or ice cream, to serve

On a well-floured surface, roll out the pastry so it's about as thick as a £1 coin, turning it 90° after each roll. This makes it easier to roll evenly and helps stop it sticking. You want to end up with a circle of pastry more than big enough to line a round 23cm (9in), loose-bottomed tart tin – taking into account the depth of the tin as well as the width.

Carefully roll one end of the pastry around your rolling pin, then lift it into the tart tin, trimming it so that it overhangs the top by a finger's width. Gently ease it into the base and corners of the tin and patch any holes with offcuts. Prick the bottom all over with a fork, then line the base and sides with a circle of baking parchment and put in the fridge for 30 minutes. Put a flat baking sheet in the oven and preheat to 190°C/375°F/Gas Mark 5.

Fill the baking parchment liner with ceramic baking beans, if you have them, or uncooked pasta shapes or rice. Put the tart tin in the oven on the preheated baking sheet and bake for 10 minutes, or until the sides have set. Remove the parchment and beans, gently moulding the pastry back up the sides with a finger if it happens to have slumped slightly.

Turn down the oven to 180°C/350°F/Gas Mark 4 and put the tart back in for 10–15 minutes, or until the shell feels dry on the bottom and is starting to turn pale golden brown. Remove from the oven and trim the top with a sharp serrated knife, then leave to cool for 10 minutes. Leave the oven on.

While the tart is cooling, beat together the butter and sugar until they're light and fluffy, then gradually beat in the eggs, one at a time, making sure each one is incorporated before you add the next. Beat in the vanilla extract, then the almonds and flour, until everything is uniformly mixed.

Sprinkle a third of the blueberries over the base of the pastry shell, then smooth the almond mixture evenly over the top. Sprinkle with the rest of the fruit, then put in the oven for 45–50 minutes, or until the almond mixture is set and golden brown. If the pastry shell looks like it's browning too quickly around the rim, make a ring of foil to cover it.

When the middle is set, remove the tart from the oven. Allow to cool a little, then carefully remove from the tin, leaving it on the metal base. Eat while still just warm, or at room temperature, sprinkling with icing sugar before serving. You might also want some thick cream, crème fraîche or vanilla ice cream.

Strawberries in red wine with cream cheese and basil

This is a freeform version of coeur à la crème, the French dessert made with a cloud of sweetened fresh cheese. The cheese is a great foil to soft summer fruit, particularly strawberries. The wine and basil syrup gives them an aromatic pepperiness.

For 4
100g (3½oz) caster sugar
150ml (5fl oz) red wine
400g (14oz) ripe strawberries, hulled and halved
8 big basil leaves

For the sweetened cream cheese
½ vanilla pod, split lengthways, or a few drops of natural vanilla extract
250g (9oz) cream cheese
250ml (9fl oz) double cream
2 tbsp caster sugar
zest of ½ lemon

Mix the sugar into the red wine until it has dissolved, then add the halved strawberries and leave in the fridge to steep for 45 minutes–1 hour.

Meanwhile, scrape the seeds from the vanilla pod and whisk into the cream cheese (or add a few drops of vanilla extract). Pour in the cream, sugar and lemon zest and whisk everything together until well combined.

Stack the basil leaves on a chopping board and roll them up to form a kind of tube. Slice across the tube with a sharp knife so that you end up with thin shreds of basil and then stir them into the strawberries.

Serve in shallow bowls, with an island of sweetened cream cheese in the middle and a moat of strawberries, basil and wine around the outside.

Strawberry and lemon curd tart

The biscuit crumb base makes this a tart in cheesecake's clothing. Needless to say, it would also work with raspberries, blueberries or blackberries – and you could substitute the lemon curd with orange.

For 6–8
250g (9oz) digestive biscuits
110g (4oz) butter
175g (6oz) good lemon curd, bought or homemade (page 216)
250g (9oz) mascarpone
500g (1lb 2oz) strawberries
1 tbsp redcurrant jelly, to glaze (optional)
a squeeze of lemon juice (optional)

Whizz the digestives to fine crumbs in a food processor, or put them in a strong polythene bag and bash vigorously with a rolling pin. Melt the butter and add the crushed digestives. Mix together well. Press firmly into a 23cm (9in), loose-bottomed tart tin, so they line the bottom and come 2cm (¾in) up the sides. Put in the fridge to chill for about 45 minutes for the crumbs to set.

Mix together the lemon curd and mascarpone until it is a smooth and uniform off-white, then pile into the tart case, spreading it out to cover the base. Hull and halve the strawberries, and arrange on top. You want the whole tart to be covered.

There's something rather nice about leaving the fruit just as it is, but if you want to glaze it, gently melt the redcurrant jelly in a small saucepan with a squeeze of lemon juice, and brush it over the top. Keep in the fridge until you're ready to eat.

Autumn mess with blackberries

This is my purple-stained autumnal take on the classic summer dessert of crushed strawberries, meringues and cream. I've included a meringue recipe, but feel free to buy them if that makes things easier. Incidentally, a bottle of crème de cassis – blackcurrant liqueur – or its blackberry cousin, crème de mûre, is a useful thing to keep in the kitchen. I slosh it over ice creams and bowls of berries, use it in jellies and sometimes add a splash or two to my gravies. It also ensures a plentiful supply of kirs or cardinals (see page 249) for summer evenings.

For 4
For the meringues
2 medium egg whites
a pinch of salt
100g (3½oz) caster sugar

For the mess
400g (14oz) blackberries
¼ tsp ground cinnamon
125ml (4fl oz) crème de cassis or, even better, crème de mûre
400ml (14fl oz) double cream
a few drops of natural vanilla extract

Start with the meringues – they'll need several hours to cook and cool. You could happily make them the day before.

Preheat the oven to 110°C/225°F/Gas Mark ¼. Any traces of grease or egg yolk will stop the egg whites from whisking properly, so wash the bowl and whisk thoroughly before you start. Cut 2 pieces of baking parchment to fit 2 baking sheets.

Put the whites in the bowl with a pinch of salt and whisk at medium speed until they form stiff peaks. When you lift the whisk, the whites should keep their peaks without flopping.

Whisking at a high speed, add 1 tbsp of the sugar and beat in for about 5 seconds. Whisk in the remaining sugar, a third at a time, then continue whisking for another 30 seconds until glossy and thick.

Use tiny dabs of the mixture at the corners of the baking sheets to keep the baking parchment in place. Use a tablespoon to make 4 equal piles of the mixture on each sheet.

cont...

Place in the oven and cook for 1¼–1½ hours, or until they lift cleanly from the baking parchment and the bottoms sound hollow when tapped. Turn off the oven and leave the meringues inside until cold.

Keep back a handful of the blackberries, then lightly squash the rest with a fork. You want a mix of mush and semi-intact fruit. Add the cinnamon and half the crème de mûre or cassis.

Beat the cream to a soft cloud with a bit of vanilla. It should be foppish and floppy rather than regimentally stiff. Crumble in chunks of meringue, add the mixed crushed berries and fold loosely together. Divide between 4 bowls or glasses, scatter with the few remaining whole berries and dribble a bit of the crème de mûre or cassis over the top.

Cherrymisu

A fruity trifle, inspired by a tiramisu-like layering of dipped sponge fingers and cream. The crumbled amaretti biscuits add a hint of bitterness, making the sweet cherries taste almost like morellos.

For 6
450g (1lb) black cherries
200ml (7fl oz) ruby port
150g (5½oz) caster sugar
4 egg yolks
300g (10½oz) mascarpone
100ml (3½fl oz) double cream
24–30 sponge fingers
6 amaretti biscuits
a pinch of ground cinnamon
a few squares of dark chocolate

Set aside six cherries for decoration. Pit and chop the rest, place in a pan with the port and 50g (1¾oz) sugar, and bring to a simmer. Remove from the heat, then strain. Cool the liquid and cherries separately.

Using an electric beater, whisk the yolks with the remaining sugar until the mixture is frothy and pale – this takes a couple of minutes. Add the mascarpone and whisk in until smooth. In another bowl, whisk the cream to soft peaks, then gently fold into the mascarpone mixture. Put in the fridge to chill for a couple of hours.

Pour the port into a shallow bowl and dip the sponge fingers into it for 10 seconds each side, or until the surface softens and colours. Layer in a shallow gratin dish, about 23 x 23cm (9 x 9in), or divide between six individual bowls or glasses, starting with the sponge fingers. Crumble over half the amaretti, then top with half the cherries and half the mascarpone mixture. Repeat with the remaining amaretti, cherries and mascarpone. Sprinkle a pinch of ground cinnamon evenly over the top, then grate over a bit of dark chocolate. Decorate with the whole cherries and chill in the fridge for at least 4 hours.

Kir and raspberry jellies

Part of the joy here is the way in which the raspberries are suspended in the jellies like lobed jewels, but if you want an easy life, just make plain kir jellies and scatter the berries around the outside.

For 6–8
7 leaves of gelatine
200ml (7fl oz) water
175g (6oz) caster sugar
5 tbsp crème de cassis
500ml (18fl oz) dry white or rosé wine, chilled
150g (5½oz) raspberries, plus a few extra for decoration
cream or vanilla ice cream, to serve

Put the gelatine in a small bowl of cold water, cutting it into pieces so it is all completely submerged, and leave to soften for 5 minutes.

Meanwhile, put the 200ml (7fl oz) water in a saucepan with the sugar and bring to a simmer, stirring until the sugar has dissolved. Remove from the heat and leave to stand for a minute. Squeeze the gelatine between your hands to get rid of the water, then stir into the sugar syrup.

When it's well combined, stir in the cassis and leave to cool to room temperature for about 45 minutes. Finally, stir in the chilled wine.

Put 1 tbsp of the jelly mixture in the bottom of six 150ml (5fl oz) jelly moulds or dariole moulds, then arrange the raspberries in a circle on top, pointed side down. Add just enough jelly to form a thin layer between the fruit and the side of the mould and place in the fridge for about 2 hours, or until the jelly is firm enough to hold the fruit in place. Leave the remaining jelly at room temperature.

When the fruit is set, top up the moulds with the remaining jelly and return to the fridge for at least 6 hours or overnight.

Turn out onto small plates and serve with cream or vanilla ice cream, adding a scattering of extra raspberries if you feel so inclined.

Funny how we think of pheasants as posh grub. Chaps with guns pay through the nose to take a pop at them, so we assume the birds themselves must be somehow rarefied and expensive. In fact, some bits of the countryside are positively overrun with the things and you can often buy four for less than the price of a good chicken. My parents' garden in Somerset is regularly invaded by strutting escapees from the local shoot, so much so that my mum has taken to standing by the window and madly flapping her arms in an attempt to drive them away. The pheasants don't seem to take much notice: they probably think she's one of them.

The upside of this pheasant glut, of course, is that they are pretty easy to get your hands on. The same goes for partridge – a perfect single-portion roast – which, like pheasant, has a subtle gamey flavour and the lean flesh you only get from birds that have flexed their muscles in the wild. Both put in an appearance at the bigger supermarkets when they're in season.

In fact, the availability of birds and poultry in general seems far better than it used to be. I'm not persuaded by the proliferation of turkey 'products' – particularly drumsticks, which look like fleshy, anaemic clubs – but being able to buy a well-bred duck, a guinea fowl and occasionally even a few quail in the aisles of a supermarket makes life a lot more interesting.

A bowl of
roast quails with
spiced yoghurt

Duck with apples
and shallots

Guinea fowl
with mushrooms
and marsala

Pot-roast pheasant
with red cabbage

Chicken schnitzel
with lemon
and thyme

Roast partridge
with bread sauce
and Madeira gravy

Birds

A bowl of roast quails with spiced yoghurt

I once made a bowl of roast quails for my book group. Since then, I seem to have gained rather a reputation for 'doing bowls'. It's a relaxed way of serving things: you just plonk the bowl on the table and let people sort themselves out.

This only needs good bread and some sort of green salad and you're all set, although a bowl of Coucous Salad with Dried Figs and Orange (page 67) would also be a nice thought.

For 4–6
150ml (5fl oz) olive oil
4 garlic cloves, crushed
2 tbsp ground cumin
1 tbsp sweet (mild) paprika
½ tsp cayenne pepper
juice of 2 lemons
salt
12 oven-ready quail
350ml (12fl oz) Greek yoghurt
2 big handfuls of coriander leaves
splash of milk

Mix the oil, garlic and spices with the juice of 1 lemon and a good sprinkling of salt. Put three-quarters of the mixture into a mixing bowl large enough to hold all the quail, add the birds and toss everything together. Cover and leave to marinate for 1 hour, turning everything over in the spice mixture occasionally.

Add the rest of the mixture to the yoghurt with a couple of decent pinches of salt, the coarsely chopped coriander leaves and as much of the remaining lemon juice as you think it needs – you may not want it all. Thin a little with a splash of milk, then put it in the fridge while you cook the quail.

Preheat the oven to 220°C/425°F/Gas Mark 7. Give the birds a final toss in the marinade, then scoop them out and pin the legs together with wooden toothpicks. Arrange in two roasting tins, leaving a bit of space between the birds so they roast rather than steam. Sprinkle generously with more salt flakes and put in the oven for 25–30 minutes, or until the skin is puffed and crisp and the legs pull away easily from the body.

Tip into a large serving bowl or plate, pour over any juices from the roasting tins and sprinkle with salt flakes. Eat with the yoghurt, your fingers and appetite.

Duck with apples and shallots

All sorts of pleasures here: crisp skin, soft fruit and a sweetly rich sauce with gentle hints of spice. Eat it with mash, roast potatoes, or – my preference – a simple tuft of watercress.

For 4
16 small round shallots, peeled
olive oil
4 duck legs
salt and pepper
2 big sprigs of rosemary
3 star anise
1 cinnamon stick, halved
4 eating apples, cored and quartered
200ml (7fl oz) dry white wine
1 tbsp runny honey

Preheat the oven to 240°C/475°F/Gas Mark 9.

Peel the shallots. This is a lot easier if you throw them into a pan of boiling water for a minute, then drain in a colander or sieve and run under the cold tap for 30 seconds or so to stop them cooking. The skins should peel off easily. Put them in a small bowl and toss with a splash of olive oil.

Rub the duck legs all over with olive oil and season well, being particularly generous with the salt. Scatter the herbs and spices over the base of a roasting tin and place the duck legs on top. Add the shallots and put the tin in the oven, turning it down to 180°C/350°F/Gas Mark 4. Cook for 30 minutes, baste the duck, and tip off all but 2 tablespoons of the fat. Add the apples, toss in the fat, and cook for another 30 minutes.

Tip off the fat again, leaving behind any dark sauce and goo. Stir in the wine and honey, scraping any bits from the bottom, then put everything back in the oven for another 15 minutes. Check the seasoning and serve.

Guinea fowl with mushrooms and marsala

I always think guinea fowl is how chicken ought to taste. The flesh is meatier than all but the most liberated of free-range birds. French farmers usually have a few pecking around their farmyards – they're notoriously good guard-dogs, as well as being good for the pot – but for some reason they're less popular in Britain. If you can't get guinea fowl, use similar pieces of chicken – or 4 chicken drumsticks and 4 thighs.

For 4
2 handfuls of dried wild mushrooms (chanterelles, morels, porcini or a mix)
300ml (10fl oz) hot chicken stock
1 decent-sized guinea fowl (about 1.25–1.5kg), cut into eight pieces: thighs, drumsticks, and 4 bits of breast, 2 with the wings attached
salt and pepper
butter
olive oil
1 big banana shallot (or 3 small round ones), finely chopped
2 garlic cloves, finely chopped
150g (5½oz) small chestnut mushrooms, roughly sliced
4 sprigs of thyme, leaves only
150ml (5fl oz) marsala (or port)
5 tbsp double cream
small handful of parsley, chopped

Put the dried wild mushrooms in a bowl, pour over the hot stock, stir and leave to soak for 30–60 minutes until soft. (It should tell you the exact soaking time on the packet.) When they have softened, squeeze the juice back into the stock, and remove the mushrooms. Keep both stock and mushrooms to one side.

Season the pieces of guinea fowl. Heat a small knob of butter and a good glug of oil in a large frying pan (ideally one that has a lid – you'll need it later – though you can use a sheet of foil instead). Add half the birdy bits and cook over a medium heat until a good golden brown on all sides – it should take 6–8 minutes in all. Shift the cooked guinea fowl to a bowl, then repeat with the remaining bits, adding a bit more butter and oil if necessary.

Remove the second lot of guinea fowl and tip out all but 1 tablespoon or so of the oil. Throw the shallots and garlic into the pan and stir for about 1 minute until they start to soften. Add another knob of butter, plus the wild and chestnut mushrooms and thyme, and cook for another couple of minutes, stirring occasionally until the mushrooms have softened, then turn up the heat, throw in the booze and bubble for a minute or so more.

cont...

Return the guinea fowl pieces to the pan and pour in the stock. Cover tightly with a lid (or a big sheet of foil) and simmer gently for 25 minutes.

Remove the guinea fowl and mushrooms with a slotted spoon and put them in a bowl – don't worry about leaving the odd bit of mushroom in the pan. Turn up the heat under the juices in the pan and bubble, uncovered, for 5–6 minutes until the sauce has thickened. Stir in any juices that have gathered under the guinea fowl and mushrooms, followed by the cream, and let everything bubble away for a minute or so. Season well, then turn down the heat, add the guinea fowl and mushrooms, and gently reheat. Scatter with parsley and serve with mash or rice in winter or a simple salad of Cos lettuce in summer.

Pot-roast pheasant with red cabbage

This smells and tastes the way winter food should, the cabbage and spices infusing the birds with flavour as they cook. The liquid keeps everything well lubricated, so you avoid the usual roast pheasant problem, a choice between dry breasts and tough sinewy legs. A mound of mash would be good on the side.

For 4
2 young, oven-ready pheasants (650–700g/1lb 7oz–1lb 9oz each)
salt and pepper
500g (1lb 2oz) red cabbage
2 eating apples
2 sprigs of thyme
butter
olive oil
125g (4½oz) streaky bacon
2 medium onions, thinly sliced
2 plump garlic cloves, chopped
8 juniper berries, crushed
1 strip of orange peel, about 5–6cm (2–2½in) long
1 bay leaf
175ml (6fl oz) red wine
3 heaped tbsp redcurrant jelly
2 tbsp red wine vinegar

Preheat the oven to 180°C/350°F/Gas Mark 4. Season the pheasants inside and out with a good sprinkling of salt and pepper. Remove the hard core from the cabbage and thinly shred the leaves. Peel and core the apples. Slice one apple thinly into rings and add to the cabbage; put half the other apple inside each pheasant, along with a sprig of thyme.

cont...

On the hob, heat a knob of butter and a glug of oil in a heavy metal casserole dish large enough to hold both pheasants, with a couple of inches to spare above them. Brown the birds well on all sides, one at a time. Remove the pheasants from the casserole dish and put to one side.

Keep back 2 rashers of the bacon, then chop the rest into strips and add to the fat. Cook for a few minutes until the bacon starts to brown, add the onions, garlic, juniper, orange peel and bay leaf, then sweat for 5 minutes, stirring occasionally until the onion is soft. Add the cabbage and apple, then cook for 20 minutes, stirring every few minutes to stop it burning. Mix in the wine and redcurrant jelly, season and bring to a simmer. Place the pheasants, breast side down, on top of the cabbage, cover and cook in the oven for 40 minutes.

Now remove the lid and stir the vinegar into the cabbage. Turn the pheasants breast side up. Cut the remaining bacon into 3 or 4 pieces, spread them a little by bashing with your fist, then drape over the pheasant breasts. Return the dish to the oven, without the lid, for 20 minutes. The pheasants are done when the legs pull away easily from the carcass. Lift the birds out at the table and carve.

Chicken schnitzel with lemon and thyme

Schnitzel, escalope, call it what you will – the combination of chicken breast and herbed crumbs is plate-lickingly good. Try to resist the temptation to give the chicken an extra couple of minutes in the pan; if you beat it thin enough, it will be cooked through.

For 4
4 skinless, boneless chicken breasts
salt and pepper
1 lemon
150g (5½oz) fine, dry breadcrumbs (dry them out in a low oven for a few
   minutes if necessary)
leaves from 10 single sprigs of thyme, finely chopped
2 tbsp plain flour
2 eggs, beaten
4 tbsp oil
50g (1¾oz) butter, plus a couple of knobs extra
salt

Preheat the oven to 110°C/225°F/Gas Mark ¼.

Cover a chopping board with a piece of clingfilm and place one of the chicken breasts on top. Cover with another sheet of clingfilm, then, using the side of a rolling pin, the flat side of a meat mallet or some other cosh-like object, beat the chicken with a firm hand until it is flattened to an even thickness of 5mm (¼in). Season generously with salt and pepper, then give the other breasts the same treatment.

Finely grate the zest of the lemon into the breadcrumbs, then mix in the thyme leaves. Lay out three plates. Put the flour on the first, the beaten egg on the second and the breadcrumbs on the third. One at a time, lay the breasts gently in the flour on both sides, so they are lightly covered all over. Shake to get rid of any excess. Now dip both sides in the egg, then into the breadcrumbs, pressing them on with your fingers to help them stick. Cover the remaining breasts in the same way.

Heat 1 tablespoon of the oil and a quarter of the butter in a frying pan over a medium heat. Add one of the breasts to the pan and cook for 2–3 minutes on each side until the crumbs are golden brown and the chicken is just cooked through. Move it onto a baking tray and place in the oven to keep warm. Wipe out any burnt bits from the pan, then repeat with the other breasts.

When all the breasts have been browned, wipe out the pan again, add a couple of big knobs of butter and let them melt and froth. Pour the bubbling butter over the schnitzels, adding a sprinkling of sea salt and a generous squeeze of juice from the lemon before you tuck in.

Roast partridge with bread sauce and Madeira gravy

A simple classic for autumn and early winter. Though the partridge season runs from 1 September until 1 February, the birds can be hard to get hold of beyond December – in any case, by then they are probably better left for the braising pot than the roasting tin. Make the bread sauce ahead of time and keep it warm. Braised red cabbage, roast potatoes or an earthy gratin would make good accompaniments.

For 4
Bread sauce
4 cloves
1 onion, peeled and halved
3 small round shallots, finely chopped
8 black peppercorns
1 bay leaf
1 blade mace
a good grating of nutmeg
300ml (10fl oz) whole milk
60g (2¼oz) white breadcrumbs
25g (1oz) butter
3–4 tbsp double cream
salt and pepper

For the partridges
4 oven-ready partridges (about 300g (10½oz) each)
salt and pepper
4 sprigs of thyme
4 garlic cloves, peeled and flattened
a few knobs of butter
olive oil
8 rashers streaky bacon
100ml (3½fl oz) rich Madeira
250ml (9fl oz) chicken stock

Start with the bread sauce. Push the cloves into the cut side of the onion halves, then put them, clove-side down, in a small saucepan with the shallots, peppercorns, bay leaf, mace, nutmeg and milk. Bring to the boil, then turn off the heat and leave to infuse for at least 45 minutes.

Remove the onion from the milk, then pick out the mace and peppercorns (leave the chopped shallots for texture). Return to the pan, with the bay leaf, add the breadcrumbs and stir over a gentle heat for about 10 minutes, until the breadcrumbs have swollen and turned the sauce thick. Beat in the butter and cream, then season generously to taste with salt, pepper and more nutmeg if you fancy it. Keep to one side with a lid on and reheat gently, without boiling, just before you want to eat.

Preheat the oven to 220°C/425°F/Gas Mark 7.

Season the partridges inside and out. Push a sprig of thyme and a clove of garlic inside each one, along with a knob of butter.

Put a shallow roasting tin on the hob – it needs to be big enough to hold all the birds with plenty of room around them. Add a couple of big knobs of butter and 2 tablespoons of oil and heat until the butter is bubbling. Add the birds, breast down, and cook for 1½ minutes on each breast until golden brown.

Switch off the heat and turn the birds breast up. Baste the breasts with the melted butter from the tin, then drape them with the bacon pieces. Put the birds in the oven – breast side up – and roast for 20 minutes.

The birds might still be a little bloody between thigh and body – that's as it should be, but give them 5–10 minutes more if it's likely to give you nightmares, or your partridges are particularly large. Once the birds are done, remove from the oven and leave to rest on a plate, breast side down, for about 10 minutes, loosely draped with a tent of foil.

While the partridges are resting, make the gravy. Put the roasting tin on the hob and tip in the Madeira. Let it bubble away for a minute or two until it thickens slightly, stirring and scraping to get all the good bits off the bottom of the pan. Then tip in the chicken stock and let everything bubble away for a few minutes more until the sauce has thickened. Stir in any resting juices, taste and season. Eat the partridges with the bacon, gravy and bread sauce.

There's a festival I go to most summers. It's a gentle, bohemian thing, based around books and writers, with good music, decent food and a bit of drinking thrown in.

There was a new attraction last time I went. The local Women's Institute had set up a trestle table and was selling its homemade cakes: lemon drizzle, sticky ginger, coffee and walnut, carrot cake and traditional fruit cake. It was doing a roaring trade, not least with me. Somehow, cake is exactly what you want when there's an evening of rap poets and merriment ahead.

It's probably sacrilegious to say so, but I've never been a huge fan of a basic Victoria sponge. My own cake-making efforts tend to be at the squidgier end of the spectrum, the sort of things you can have for dinner as well as for tea. I usually replace at least part of the flour with ground almonds, which I think gives a richer flavour and more satisfying texture, and sometimes dispense with it altogether. Chocolate sponge, in particular, can be depressingly dry and dull if it's too heavy on the flour, which is why my own chocolate cake is of the dense, dark, flourless variety. It's not particularly traditional, but I like to think the WI would approve, nonetheless.

Cakes

Go-with-anything cake

This was the subject of one of the first newspaper food columns I ever wrote. It's sticky and dense and sweet – a safe bet when you need something to round off supper. It genuinely does go with pretty much anything: fruit compôte, a scattering of fresh fruit, a blob of cream or ice cream, a few slices of sweet orange…

Anyone worried about gluten or fat might also like to know that it contains neither flour nor butter.

For 6
3 medium eggs
150g (5½oz) caster sugar
175g (6oz) ground almonds
zest and juice of ½ lemon
¼–½ tsp ground cinnamon
icing sugar, to dust

Preheat the oven to 180°C/350°F/Gas Mark 4. Butter a shallow 18cm (7in) round cake tin. Cut a piece of greaseproof paper to fit the bottom and push it in.

Separate the eggs: whites in one mixing bowl, yolks in another. With a wooden spoon, beat the yolks with 125g (4½oz) of the sugar until pale and creamy. Fold in the ground almonds, zest, juice and cinnamon to make a stiff paste.

Using a clean whisk (an electric one, preferably, to spare your arms), whisk the whites until they form soft peaks – the tops will droop when you lift the beaters. When they're peaking, gradually whisk in the remaining sugar. Keep whisking until the mixture is glossy and the peaks are stiff when you remove the whisk.

Stir one-third of the whisked whites into the almond mixture to loosen it slightly, then, using a metal spoon, carefully fold in the remaining mixture, in two batches. Be gentle – and don't worry if there are a few flecks of white left in the mixture. Better that than to lose all the air you've whisked in.

Transfer the mixture to the tin and bake in the preheated oven for 35 minutes. Provided you switched on the oven to the right temperature and gave it time to heat up beforehand, the cake should be done; a bit of squidge one way or the other doesn't really matter. It should be lightly risen, with a chewy crust, but still quite soft inside. It will be a darker brown around the edge than in the middle. If you're worried it might burn – I don't know your oven – you could always cover it with foil for the last 5–10 minutes.

cont…

Leave it to cool a little. It will probably sink or crack slightly, but don't worry – just call it rustic charm. Then turn out the cake, remove the greaseproof circle and flip it onto a plate so that the brown side faces upwards. Sift some icing sugar over the top and serve while still slightly warm.

Little almond cakes with raspberries

These are sweet, soft, moreish and almost imbecilically easy to make. Feel free to adapt them as you see fit, spiking them with vanilla instead of lemon zest or replacing the raspberries with blackberries, blueberries or blackcurrants. Personally, I'd avoid strawberries – I'm never convinced that cooked strawberries are a good thing.

Makes 12
175g (6oz) butter, plus extra for greasing
250g (9oz) icing sugar, plus extra for dusting
140g (5oz) ground almonds
60g (2¼oz) plain flour
finely grated zest of 1 lemon
5 medium egg whites
12 raspberries

Preheat the oven to 180°C/350°F/Gas Mark 4. Generously grease a nonstick 12-hole muffin tin with butter. (Mine has holes about 7cm/2¾in wide and about 2cm/¾in deep.)

Melt the butter in a pan over a low heat until it bubbles and froths. Put the 250g (9oz) icing sugar, almonds, flour and lemon zest in a bowl and mix together well. Stir in the egg whites, then beat vigorously for about 10 seconds. Pour on the melted butter and beat until everything is thoroughly combined. It should be a smooth batter.

Divide the mixture evenly between the muffin holes and put a berry on the top of each cake. You don't need to press it in – it will sink in as it cooks. Put the tin in the oven and bake for 20 minutes. The cakes will rise above their holes and puff up irregularly in the middle. You want them to be golden brown at the edges. They may still be a bit unset around the fruit, but they will firm up as they cool.

Eat while still just warm or at room temperature, sifting an ethereal dusting of icing sugar over the top before you indulge.

Apple and sultana cake

Strudelish flavours cushioned between layers of buttery sponge. This is as good for pudding as it is for teatime.

For 4–6
125g (4½oz) butter, plus extra for greasing
125g (4½oz) light brown or light muscovado sugar
125g (4½oz) self-raising flour
1 medium egg
200g (7oz) Bramley apples (1–2 depending on size)
2 handfuls of sultanas
finely grated zest of 1 small lemon
½ tsp ground cinnamon
fresh nutmeg
a handful of flaked almonds

Preheat the oven to 180°C/350°F/Gas Mark 4. Grease an 18cm (7in) cake tin and line the bottom with a circle of baking parchment.

Put the butter and 100g (3½oz) sugar in a saucepan and stir over a gentle heat until the butter has melted and the sugar dissolved. Quickly stir in the flour and beat in the egg. You'll end up with something that looks like what it is – flour mixed with melted butter – rather than normal cake mixture. Don't worry, it's meant to look like that.

Spread half the mixture over the bottom of the cake tin, then arrange the apple slices on top. Scatter with 3 tablespoons sugar, then add the sultanas, lemon zest and spices (you want to grate in about one-eighth of a whole nutmeg). Spread the remaining cake mixture over the top, smoothing it out as best you can. Scatter with the flaked almonds and put the tin in the oven for 35–40 minutes, or until it's a deep gold and firm to the touch.

Have a look after 30 minutes and cover the top with a bit of foil if it's browning too quickly. Remove from the oven and leave to stand in the tin for 10 minutes, then turn out and cool on a rack for at least quarter of an hour. It's best while still just warm.

Chocolate marmalade slump cake

This is a slim, grown-up, end-of-dinner type cake rather than something big and blowsy for teatime. It rises as it cooks, then sinks to give a dense, rich brownie-like centre, flavoured with a hint of orange. Some sort of cream to go with it is pretty much compulsory.

Makes a 23cm (9in) round cake
100g (3½oz) good Seville orange marmalade, with lots of chunky peel
finely grated zest of 1 large orange
125g (4½oz) caster sugar
150g (5½oz) unsalted butter
150g (5½oz) good dark chocolate (60–70% cocoa solids), broken into bits
4 medium eggs, separated
a pinch of salt
50g (1¾oz) cocoa powder
icing sugar, for dusting

Preheat the oven to 190°C/375°F/Gas Mark 5. Line the bottom of a round, loose-bottomed 23cm (9in) tin with a circle of baking parchment, and cut a long strip about 4cm (1½in) wide to make a collar around the inside.

Put the marmalade and zest in a food processor and blitz to a slush. Add the sugar and whizz in.

Put the butter in a small saucepan and melt over a gentle heat. Remove from the hob and leave to stand for a couple of minutes, then throw in the chocolate, pushing it under so it's just submerged. Leave to melt without stirring for about 3 minutes, then mix until smooth and glossy. Stir in the marmalade and orange zest slush and tip into a bowl.

Beat the egg yolks vigorously into the chocolate mixture, then sift the cocoa powder over the top and beat that in as well. Put the whites in a clean metal mixing bowl with a pinch of salt and, using a scrupulously clean whisk, whip until they form soft peaks – they should flop over at the top when you lift the whisk. Beat a third of the whisked egg whites into the chocolate mixture to loosen it a little, then carefully fold in the rest, scooping the chocolatey goo from the bottom of the bowl as you go, until it's a uniform brown.

cont…

Pour the mixture into the lined tin, smooth the top and bake in the oven for 30 minutes, or until the centre has risen to form a set and slightly undulating plateau. Remove from the oven and leave to cool for at least 15 minutes, then carefully take it out of the tin on its base and peel the paper from around the sides (I just deal with the paper on the bottom when I come to slice it) Leave to cool until just warm – about 30 minutes out of the oven – or room temperature.

Just before serving, sift a bit of icing sugar over the top. Serve in slices with double cream, crème fraîche, ice cream or mascarpone.

Lemon and cardamom drizzle cake

I'm rather pleased with this. I came up with it one afternoon when I felt the need for something extra in my drizzle cake. The flavour is familiar yet exotic.

For 6–8
175g (6oz) butter, softened, plus extra for greasing
1½ tbsp green cardamom pods
175g (6oz) self-raising flour
1 tsp baking powder
175g (6oz) light muscovado or light brown sugar
finely grated zest of 4 lemons and juice of 2
3 medium eggs, at room temperature, lightly beaten
50g (1¾oz) granulated sugar

Preheat the oven to 180°C/350°F/Gas Mark 4. Generously grease a 21 x 10cm/ 8¼ x 4in (900g/2lb) loaf tin, then cut a strip of baking parchment long and wide enough to line the bottom and ends. Press it into the tin.

Slit the cardamom pods open with a sharp knife and shake or poke out the dark seeds. This takes a few minutes, though it isn't particularly onerous. Put the seeds in a pestle and mortar and crush them to a coarse powder (or chop them with a knife on a chopping board).

Sift the flour and the baking powder into a bowl. Put the butter and muscovado sugar in a mixing bowl with the crushed cardamom seeds and half the lemon zest, and cream together with electric beaters, or a wooden spoon, until fluffy and smooth. Beat in the eggs, a splash or two at a time, making sure each bit is fully incorporated before you add the next. If it starts to curdle, beat in 1 tablespoon of the flour to bring it back together.

Fold in the flour until the mixture is smooth, then quickly beat in half the lemon juice. Tip into the lined loaf tin and smooth the top, then put into the oven and bake for 40 minutes, or until set and golden brown.

While the cake is still hot, spike the top about 20 times with a fork. Mix together the remaining lemon juice and zest, then quickly stir in the granulated sugar, without letting it dissolve too much, and spoon over the top, guiding the liquid towards the holes. Leave to cool completely in the tin before serving.

As children, my sister and I had a pet lamb. We were there when he was born and christened him Skippety. The grown-ups, somewhat more prosaically, called him Lamb Chop. A few months later, their name proved far more apposite than ours. We cried for hours, but had to admit that he tasted rather good.

It clearly did me no lasting damage. I have a huge fondness for lamb chops and often throw a few under a hot grill for supper. With a marinade of garlic, oregano, lemon and thyme, the smell flies you instantly to the Aegean. They're even better dipped in a bowl of tzatziki.

You can get chops from almost any animal, though we don't always call them that. A chop is pretty much anything that's cut at right angles to the backbone. A T-bone steak is actually a chop. A rack of venison is just lots of them joined together.

There's always a good selection at my local butcher's: thick pork chops with a bit of kidney attached; pale pink veal chops with creamy white fat; lamb loin chops and neat little cutlets; double-sided Barnsley chops that look like full Edwardian moustaches; and the King of Chops, the single rib of beef, its bone scraped clean, the meat trimmed and tied. It looks rather like a big lollipop and is just as much of a pleasure to eat.

Lamb cutlets
in breadcrumbs
with anchovy
and basil sauce

Pork chops
with mustard
and capers

Spiced rack
of lamb with
butter bean mash

Veal chops
with Roquefort
and thyme butter

Beef chop with
Chimmichuri
or Béarnaise

Chops

Lamb cutlets in breadcrumbs with anchovy and basil sauce

I've always liked the way that lamb cutlets have a ready-made bone handle – there's a particular pleasure to be had from things you can eat with your hands. But it's the contrast of crisp crumbs and blushing pink meat that's particularly winning here. You want the cutlets 'frenched': trimmed of the top wedge of fat, so there's virtually no fat covering the nugget of meat and with the bones scraped clean. I think a green salad is all you need to go with this, though you might also want some simple, sautéed potatoes.

For 4

12 lamb cutlets, french-trimmed
salt and pepper
2 sprigs rosemary, leaves only, very finely chopped
150g (5½oz) fine, dry breadcrumbs (dry them out in a low oven for a few
    minutes if necessary)
a few tbsp plain flour
3 medium eggs, beaten
vegetable oil, for frying
butter

If the cutlets haven't been 'frenched', trim away the fat covering the meat, and scrape the bones clean with a sharp knife. Next, flatten the meaty bit of each cutlet a little – I use the side of my fist – and season on both sides. Mix the rosemary with the crumbs.

Lay out three plates. Put the flour on the first, seasoning generously with salt and pepper, put the beaten egg on the second and the breadcrumb mixture on the third.

One at a time, lay the meaty bit of the cutlets gently in the flour on both sides, so they are lightly dusted all over, and shake to get rid of any excess flour. Now dip both sides in the egg, then into the breadcrumbs, pressing them on with your fingers to help them stick. Put on a plate and keep to one side while you crumb the other cutlets.

You'll need a couple of big frying pans to cook them all at the same time, though you could do them in two batches and keep the first lot warm in a low oven while you cook the others.

cont…

Pour 2 tablespoons of oil into each pan and heat over a medium heat. You want it hot enough to sizzle when you drop in a pinch of breadcrumbs. Add the cutlets and cook for about 2½ minutes, or until the crumbs are golden brown, then turn onto the other side and add a big knob of butter to each pan, letting it melt under and around the cutlets. Give them 2½ minutes more, then remove from the pans, draining them briefly on crumpled kitchen towel. Season with a sprinkling of salt flakes.

They're delicious with a simple squeeze of lemon, but even better if you have something to dip them in: mayonnaise, aioli, salsa verde (page 255), tzatziki or this moreishly savoury anchovy and basil sauce.

Anchovy and basil sauce
1 small garlic clove, crushed
8 anchovy fillets in olive oil (brown, not white ones)
2 egg yolks
½ tsp Dijon mustard
1 tbsp red wine vinegar
salt and pepper
150ml (5fl oz) vegetable oil
2 tbsp extra-virgin olive oil
a small handful of basil leaves, chopped

In a small food processor or pestle and mortar, blend the garlic and 6 of the anchovy fillets (without the oil from the tin) to give a smooth, salty paste. Put into a small bowl with the egg yolks, mustard, vinegar and seasoning, then stir everything together. Next, gradually beat in the oils, a drop at a time at first, to give a thick sauce. Finely chop the remaining anchovies and stir in, along with the basil leaves.

Pork chops with mustard and capers

It was grub like this that got me into French food. You used to find something similar at every truck stop café on every Route Nationale. I think you probably still do. This just needs a crisp green salad on the side – some crunchy Cos lettuce with mustard dressing, perhaps – and maybe a bit of mash for mopping. Mustard sauce, incidentally, works well with most kinds of white meat: chicken and rabbit as well as pork.

For 4

4 good pork chops, about 2–3cm (¾–1¼in) thick, preferably on the bone
salt and pepper
leaves from 4 bushy sprigs of thyme
olive oil
2 garlic cloves, crushed
150ml (5fl oz) dry white wine
250ml (9fl oz) chicken stock
150ml (5fl oz) double cream
2 tbsp capers, rinsed and drained if salted, or with the vinegar squeezed out
1 heaped tbsp Dijon mustard
a handful of chopped parsley

If the chops still have their skin on, cut it off, leaving about 1cm (½in) of fat along the outside. Cut into the fat in a few places – this will help it cook through. Scatter the chops with salt, pepper, half the thyme leaves and a splash of olive oil. Rub everything in well and leave to one side for 30 minutes if you have time.

Preheat the oven to 220°C/425°F/Gas Mark 7.

When you're ready to cook, heat a large frying pan for a few minutes to get it hot. Lay the pork chops into the hot pan and sear for 1½–2 minutes on each side to brown the surface. Next, up-end them onto their fat edge and cook for a minute or two more to crisp the fat.

Take the chops from the pan and put them in a shallow roasting tin. Keep the frying pan to one side. Put the chops in the oven for 8–10 minutes, depending on their thickness, until they are cooked through. Check the juices, but don't torture them with overcooking. Remove and cover with foil to keep warm.

Meanwhile, put the frying pan back on the hob over a medium heat and throw the garlic and remaining thyme into the fat. Stir for a couple of seconds, then add the wine and stock. Let everything bubble away for 5 minutes, or until it's thick and syrupy. Tip in any juices from the roasting tin, then add the cream, capers and mustard. Bubble for a minute or two more to thicken, then stir in the parsley and pour over the waiting chops.

Spiced rack of lamb with butter bean mash

You want a rack of lamb that has been 'frenched' by the butcher, so the bones are clean and there is no fat covering the nugget of flesh. If it is still topped by a thick pad of fatty meat, peel it off, using a small, sharp knife to help it along if necessary.

Weigh the racks, which can vary hugely in size. Largish ones will each be 500–600g (1lb 2oz–1lb 5oz) once they are trimmed, medium ones 300–400g (10½–14oz) and small ones 250–300g (9–10½oz). Work out which yours are – it will determine how long you cook them.

For 4
2 racks of lamb (6–8 bones each), french-trimmed (see above)
1 tsp crushed chilli flakes
1 tsp sweet (mild) paprika
5 garlic cloves, crushed
4 tsp ground cumin
2 lemons
150ml (5fl oz) extra-virgin olive oil, plus extra for dressing
salt and pepper
2 x 400g (14oz) cans butter beans
3 big handfuls of fresh coriander, chopped
350ml (12fl oz) Greek yoghurt
4 handfuls of baby salad leaves

Cut each rack in half so you have 4 lots of 3–4 ribs. In a large mixing bowl, stir together the chilli, paprika, 3 of the crushed garlic cloves, 2 teaspoons of the cumin, the juice of ½ lemon and 4 tablespoons of the oil. Toss the racks in the mixture until they're well coated, then leave to one side for at least 30 minutes, or a few hours if you have time.

Preheat the oven to 220°C/425°F/Gas Mark 7. Heat a large ovenproof frying pan (or heavy roasting tin) on the hob for about 5 minutes, without any oil. Season the lamb and add it to the pan, meaty side down – it should sizzle if the pan is hot enough. Leave it to brown for 2 minutes, then turn over and cook the underside for a minute or so, followed by 30 seconds on each end.

Balance the racks on their bones in the pan, spoon the rest of the marinade over the top, and put in the oven. Cook small ones for 11–12 minutes, large ones for 16–17 minutes and medium ones for somewhere in between (this will give you meat that's on the blushing side of medium rare; leave it in for 2–5 minutes longer if you want it better done, or if the racks happen to be abnormally large).

Remove the meat from the pan, pour over any cooking juices and leave to rest for 5–10 minutes, covered by a loose tent of foil.

While the racks are in the oven, make the butter bean mash. Drain and rinse the butter beans. Put in a food processor with the remaining 2 crushed garlic cloves, 6 tablespoons oil and 2 teaspoons cumin. Add the juice of 1 lemon and a good sprinkle of salt, then blitz until smoothish, but with the odd chunky bit. You may have to scrape down the sides.

Mix the coriander leaves into the yoghurt, thinning with a few tablespoons of water or milk, so you end up with a dolloping consistency. Season well, particularly with salt. Dress the salad leaves with salt, pepper, a squeeze of lemon and a splash of olive oil.

Divide the mash between 4 bowls. Slice the racks of lamb into pink chops and top each bowl with 3–4 of them, dribbling over any juices. Add a blob or two of the yoghurt, a tuft of dressed leaves and, if you want, a squeeze more lemon juice and a glug of olive oil.

Veal chops with Roquefort and thyme butter

This is the sort of indulgent lunch I often crave, but seldom eat. I think it needs only the simplest of salads on the side: maybe a handful of watercress and some thinly sliced shallots, tossed with salt, pepper, olive oil and the merest splash of red wine vinegar. Some sauté potatoes would be a nice idea too.

Please try to use British rosé veal, which is raised to high welfare standards.

For 2
For the Roquefort butter:
150g (5½oz) butter, softened
100g (3½oz) Roquefort cheese
1 tsp thyme leaves, chopped
1 tsp smooth Dijon mustard
1 garlic clove, crushed
2 small squeezes of lemon juice

For the chops:
½ tbsp olive oil
½ tbsp butter
2 rosé veal chops, about 2.5cm (1in) thick
salt and freshly ground black pepper

cont…

To make the Roquefort butter, put the butter in a mixing bowl and beat until smooth. Add the cheese and remaining ingredients and mix to a smooth paste. (You can, of course, do all this in a food processor). Tip the mixture onto a bit of foil or clingfilm and roll into a sausage about 3cm (1¼in) across. Twist the ends so the mixture is totally enclosed, and put in the fridge or freezer to harden for at least 30 minutes. This will probably make more Roquefort butter than you need, but it's good on all sorts of steaks.

Heat a large frying pan for a few minutes over a medium high heat. Add the oil and the butter. Wait for the butter to froth, then add the chops and cook for 3 minutes each side, until golden brown, seasoning each side as you turn. When the sides are done, stand the chops on end for a minute or two so the fat can crisp up, then give them another 30 seconds or so resting on their bones. This should give you meat that is pinkly juicy in the middle.

Remove from the pan and allow to rest on warm plates for about 5 minutes. Halfway through the resting, slice a couple of rounds of Roquefort butter onto each chop so that they start to melt and mingle with the juices.

Beef chop with Chimmichurri or Béarnaise

This is a sort of super-steak – a trimmed, single rib of beef on the bone. It's what the French call 'côte de boeuf'. They vary quite a lot in weight, depending on the size of the animal. If you have difficulty tracking one down, you could always use some bits of rib eye steak instead – they will need only about 3 minutes each side in a hot pan.

I've given you a choice of sauces: the gutsy garlic and herb dressing of the Argentinian gauchos or the unctuous egg, butter and tarragon sauce of the French bistro. I think it depends what sort of mood you're in. Either way, it's a carnivorous treat. Get the sauce ready before you cook the meat.

For 3–4
1 trimmed single rib of beef on the bone (côte de boeuf), about 5cm (2in)
  thick and weighing about 1kg (2lb 4oz)
olive oil
salt and pepper
a knob of butter
1 garlic clove, flattened
2 sprigs of thyme

cont…

Preheat the oven to 220°C/425°F/Gas Mark 7.

Rub the chop all over with olive oil and season well. Heat an ovenproof frying pan until it's smoking hot. Add the beef and cook for 3 minutes each side, then add the butter, garlic and thyme and baste the chop for a few seconds. Up-end the chop and brown the edges for a minute or so, then spoon over the juices again and put the pan in the oven.

Leave it in there for 15 minutes (a 1kg/2lb 4oz chop of the specified thickness will be rare after this time: one that's half the weight will need only 8–9 minutes and a 750g/1lb 10oz chop about 12 minutes).

When the time is up, remove the pan from the oven, sprinkle the chop with a pinch more salt, then put it on a plate to rest for 15 minutes, covering it with a lose tent of foil to keep it warm.

Carve into slices parallel with the bone – the outer slices will be a little better done – and serve with one of the following sauces.

Chimmichurri

A punchy, big-flavoured sauce from Argentina, which is the country not only of gauchos, but of very small women eating very large steaks.

2 big handfuls of flatleaf parsley, finely chopped
leaves from 5 sprigs of thyme (or 1 tbsp fresh oregano, if you can find it), finely chopped
1 bay leaf, finely chopped
3 garlic cloves, crushed
a big pinch of ground cumin
a pinch of cayenne pepper
100ml (3½fl oz) extra-virgin olive oil
2 tbsp red wine vinegar
sea salt flakes and black pepper

Mix the chopped herbs, garlic, cumin and cayenne. Stir together the oil and vinegar, adding 2 tablespoons of water and ¼ teaspoon salt flakes. Mix the liquid with the herbs, add a few grinds of pepper and leave to stand for at least an hour. Check the seasoning before you serve – it could need up to ¼ teaspoon more salt.

Béarnaise

This is my simplified version of the classic egg and butter sauce, flavoured with tarragon. It's a perfect silken partner to any sort of steak.

3 sprigs of tarragon
300g (10½oz) butter
1 bay leaf
2 small shallots, thinly sliced
4 egg yolks
1 tbsp white wine vinegar
a squeeze of lemon juice
a pinch of cayenne pepper
salt and pepper

Fill a blender with just boiled water to warm it a little. Strip the leaves from the tarragon and keep to one side. Put the stalks in a small saucepan – preferably one with a spout; you'll need to pour it later – along with the butter, bay leaf and shallots. Heat gently until the butter has completely melted.

Empty the hot water from the blender and quickly shake dry. Put the yolks and vinegar in the blender and whizz together for about 30 seconds. Reheat the butter until it's hot and bubbling.

Switch on the blender and, with the motor running, very slowly strain the hot butter onto the egg yolks in a thin stream (leaving the bay and tarragon stalks and the shallots in the sieve). Don't rush: the whole pouring process should take about 20 seconds, during which time the sauce should thicken to a thin mayonnaise-like consistency. Add a squeeze of lemon, to taste, plus 1 tablespoon of hot water from the kettle and whizz again.

Chop the tarragon leaves and stir in, along with some pepper, a pinch of cayenne and a generous sprinkling of salt. It will keep warm for at least 20 minutes in a bowl suspended over a pan of hot (but turned off) water – or, even better, for several hours in a Thermos flask.

I've never met anyone who is ambivalent about fennel. Fennel is the Marmite of the vegetable world: you either love it or hate it. I think it must be genetic.

I am firmly in the fennel-loving camp. I love the aniseed flavour, which sits at the milder end of the liquorice scale – a gentle hint rather than a full-on blast. I love the contrast between the pale layers of the raw bulb and the green plume of its feathery fronds. I love the refreshing liquid crunch when it is sliced wafer-thin and, perhaps most of all, its mellow softness when cooked. Braised with butter until the bulb and its juices turn rich and sweet, fennel is arguably at its most sublime.

If you're a fennel hater, I understand if you want to turn the page. But I'd much rather you gave it a go.

Fennel, pear
and pomegranate

Braised fennel

Shaved fennel
with celery leaves
and Parmesan

Chicken with fennel,
lemon and thyme

Sea bream
with fennel and
blood orange

Fennel

Fennel, pear and pomegranate

A wonderful autumn combination, sweet and sharp and crisp, the whites and pale greens jewelled with pearls of red. I sometimes add a few blobs of soft, rindless goat's cheese, though on balance, I prefer it just as it is.

For 4
juice of ½ lemon
½ tsp Dijon mustard
1 tsp runny honey
2–3 tbsp extra-virgin olive oil
sea salt and pepper
1 large fennel bulb, with its fronds
2 ripe pears
2 big handfuls of rocket
½ pomegranate

Whisk together the lemon, mustard, honey and oil with a bit of seasoning. Be generous with the salt. Trim the fennel bulb and slice it as thinly as possible: think wafers rather than wedges. Cut the pears, unpeeled, into stickish pieces, avoiding the core, then toss everything with the dressing and rocket. Scatter over some of the pomegranate seeds, avoiding the white pith, and squeeze some of the juice over the top.

Braised fennel

I love this just as it is, with nothing more than a bit of bread for soaking up the buttery juices, but it's also great with roast pork.

For 2 as a main course, or 4 as an accompaniment
2 big or 4 small fennel bulbs, trimmed, fronds reserved
25g (1oz) butter
2 whole garlic cloves, peeled and flattened
250ml (9fl oz) chicken stock
juice of ½ lemon

Cut the fennel bulbs into quarters. Melt the butter in a wide saucepan or lidded frying pan. Add the fennel bulbs and cook over a medium heat until tinged with gold on all sides. Throw in the garlic cloves, then pour over the stock and lemon juice. Season.

Cover with a lid and cook for 30 minutes, then remove the lid and cook for 15 minutes more until the juices are thick and syrupy. Check the seasoning, then bathe the fennel in the juices, scattering the feathery fronds over the top.

Shaved fennel with celery leaves and Parmesan

This is precisely what it says it is, give or take a squeeze of lemon and a splash of oil. It's one of those perfect uncomplicated combinations. You want the fennel to be wafer-thin, so use a sharp knife, or a mandolin if you have one.

For 4

2–3 big fennel bulbs, trimmed, fronds reserved

4 handfuls of celery leaves (the pale green leaves, plucked from the very centre of a head of celery – include some of the spindly young stalks as well if you want)

juice and zest of 1 lemon

sea salt flakes and black pepper

2 handfuls of shaved Parmesan

extra-virgin olive oil

Slice the fennel as thinly as you possibly can. Put the fronds to one side. Arrange the fennel slices on a large serving plate and scatter with the celery leaves. Mix together the lemon juice and zest. Season the fennel and celery well, particularly with salt, and sprinkle with half the lemon juice mixture. Scatter with the Parmesan and splash the whole thing with a few good glugs of olive oil. Taste a bit and add more lemon if you think it needs it. Throw the fennel fronds nonchalantly over the top.

Chicken with fennel, lemon and thyme

Even if you're a fennel hater, I'd urge you to give this a go. The flavour softens with the lemon and chicken juices.

For 4

2 big or 3 small fennel bulbs
3 garlic cloves, thinly sliced
1 big lemon, thinly sliced
6 tbsp olive oil
salt and pepper
4 sprigs of thyme
8 chicken thighs, skin on
4 tbsp dry white wine

Preheat the oven to 200°C/400°F/Gas Mark 6. Trim the fennel, keeping the fronds, and slice the bulbs about 5mm (¼in) thick. Toss with the garlic, lemon and 4 tablespoons oil. Season well and spread over the bottom of a large roasting tin. Scatter with half the thyme.

Season the chicken bits and place them, skin-side up, on top of the fennel – you want to leave a bit of space between them. Splash the remaining oil over the skin, add a sprinkle more salt and scatter with the remaining thyme sprigs. Put in the oven and roast for 40 minutes, then baste with the juices, pour the wine into the tin around the chicken and turn up the heat to 240°C/475°F/Gas Mark 9. Put back in the oven and roast for another 10 minutes, or until the skin is crisp and golden.

Leave to cool for 5 minutes – the flavours come out more when it's warm rather than oven hot – then pile the fennel and lemons into wide bowls, along with a sprig of thyme. Put a couple of chicken pieces on top of each one and scatter with the fennel fronds. You might want a grind more black pepper. By the way, the lemon bits are for eating, not just flavour.

Sea bream with fennel and blood orange

This is a simple, gentle and delicious combination of flavours. In late winter and spring, when they are available, blood oranges give vivid contrasts of crimson, white and green. The Sanguinello and Moro varieties have the deepest red flesh. Use other oranges the rest of the year.

For 2
2 sea bream fillets, about 125g (4½oz) each (ask the fishmonger
  to pin-bone them)
salt and pepper
2 small blood oranges (or other oranges)
1 large fennel bulb
a big handful of basil leaves
2 tbsp finely chopped red onion
1 tbsp white wine vinegar
extra-virgin olive oil

Split the fillets in two lengthways to give four half fillets. If the fillets still have any pinbones – the tiny raised bones you can feel when you run your finger down the centre of the thick end of the fillets - you should be able to cut either side of them. Make three shallow slashes in the skin of each half fillet, season well on the flesh side, then leave to one side while you make the salad.

Cut the peel and pith from the oranges: cut off each end, then slice down around the curve of the orange to remove the remaining peel. Cut either side of the membranes that separate the segments and ease them out, getting rid of any stray pips and pith. Put the segments in a bowl along with any juices. Squeeze the juice from one of the orange membranes over the top.

Trim the fennel and slice as thinly as possible, keeping any fronds. Throw the slices into the bowl with the oranges. Tear most of the basil leaves into small pieces and add to the fennel and orange, along with the red onion. Season well with salt and pepper, then add the vinegar and a splash or two of extra-virgin olive oil. Toss together.

Heat a good splash of olive oil in a large, non-stick frying pan. Pat the skin of the fillets dry and fry for 3–4 minutes, skin side down, pressing them down gently to begin with so they don't curl up. You want the skin to be just crisp. Carefully turn them over and turn off the heat, then leave them in the pan for about 30 seconds, or until they're just cooked through. Divide the salad between 2 plates, draining off some of the liquid, and balance a couple of half fillets on top of each. Scatter any fennel fronds over the top, plus a few extra basil leaves.

There's a sign at my local greengrocer's: 'Do not squeeze the figs'. Everything about a ripe fig invites tactile exploration: the velvet skin, the raindrop plumpness, the sense of precious fragility.

But the real sensual pleasure is what's inside. The tangled mass of pink or crimson threads – not, in fact, seeds, but tiny flowers that will never blossom – has a flavour that is both distinctive and strangely intangible, a mix of leafiness and honey that echoes the perfume of a fig tree in full sun. It's this blend of sweet and green that makes figs so good with young goat's cheeses and salty blues.

Then there's the gentle crunch, a textural contrast that is amplified when the fruit are dried. The honeyed flavour condenses to a nutty toffee-ishness that's no longer fig-tree fresh but fig-roll sweet. The dried fruit naturally lends itself to cakes, jams and other sticky things – figgy pudding is a variation on the traditional Christmas pud. But it also goes particularly well with North African flavours, adding a sweet note to couscous, tagines and the like. Fresh figs, too, can be cooked with meat, especially pork or duck – or simply roasted with honey for afters.

However you eat them, they're compulsively delicious. Just resist the temptation to squeeze.

Fresh figs with
goat's cheese
and mint

Couscous salad
with dried figs
and orange

Figs with
Roquefort,
walnuts and
rosemary

Soft fig and
ginger cakes

Baked figs with
chocolate sauce
and ice cream

Figs

Fresh figs with goat's cheese and mint

I have a friend who will eat only food that contains three distinct colours. She also happens to be certifiably obsessed with purple. I think this could well be her perfect dish. You can, if you want, substitute feta for the goat's cheese, though you'll need to be less liberal with the salt. Either way, don't stint on the olive oil.

For 4
8 ripe purple figs (more if they're particularly small)
150g (5½oz) soft, mild, rindless goat's cheese
sea salt and pepper
extra-virgin olive oil
a handful of small mint leaves

Cut or tear the figs into halves or quarters and arrange them on a serving plate. Dot blobs of the goat's cheese between the fruit, then sprinkle some salt and pepper over the top. Splash with streaks of good olive oil, then scatter with mint leaves. That's it – and it's delicious.

Couscous salad with dried figs and orange

I've never been one for a rice salad. The memory of bland 1970s buffet fodder, punctuated by squares of raw green peppers and knobs of mushroom, leaves me glacially cold. I do, though, love the bulgur salads of the Middle East, speckled with a mass of finely chopped herbs, and the Moroccan idea – used more in hot dishes than cold – of mixing fragrant spice with the sweetness of dried fruit. This recipe brings them together.

For 4
300g (10½oz) couscous
450ml (16fl oz) boiling water
juice of 2 lemons
2 garlic cloves, crushed
½–1 tsp sea salt
1 tsp caster sugar
½ tsp ground cinnamon
1½ tsp ground cumin
½ tsp sweet (mild) paprika
150ml (5fl oz) extra-virgin olive oil
1 large orange
15 ready-to-eat dried figs, stalks removed, finely sliced
3 big handfuls of coriander, roughly chopped
20 large mint leaves, torn
2 handfuls of pine nuts, toasted

cont…

Put the couscous in a large heatproof bowl. Pour over the boiling water, then cover with clingfilm and leave for 30 minutes, or until all the water has been absorbed.

In a salad bowl, mix the lemon juice with the crushed garlic, salt, sugar and spices. Stir in the olive oil. Coarsely grate in the zest of the orange, avoiding the white pith. Cut off the remaining skin and, with a sharp knife, slice between the papery membranes to release the segments. Add them to the bowl and squeeze in the juice from the membranes using your hands.

Add the sliced figs, coriander, mint, pine nuts and soaked couscous to the bowl and stir well. The flavours can happily mingle for 1 hour or so before you eat.

Fresh figs with Roquefort, walnuts and rosemary

This is a marriage of contrasts: salty cheese, sweet figs and honey, the bitter crunch of walnuts and the resinous intensity of rosemary. It's moreishly good.

For 4
a big handful of chopped walnuts
1 tbsp red wine vinegar
3 tbsp runny honey
salt and pepper
2 tbsp extra-virgin olive oil
4 big or 8 small ripe purple figs
4 small handfuls of rocket
200g (7oz) Roquefort cheese
finely chopped leaves from 1 sprig of rosemary

Throw the walnuts into a frying pan – without any oil – and stir over the heat for 3–4 minutes, or until just tinged with gold. Remove and keep to one side.

In a small bowl, mix together the red wine vinegar and 2 tablespoons of the honey. Season well, then whisk in the oil.

Quarter or halve the figs and arrange them on a serving plate. Dribble the remaining honey over the top.

Toss the rocket leaves with 1 tablespoon of the dressing, and arrange casually around the figs. Top each bit of fruit with a tottering slab of the cheese, and scatter the walnuts over the plate. Splash with some of the remaining dressing – you may not need all of it – then sprinkle the rosemary over the top.

Soft fig and ginger cakes

These are deceptive little cakes. They are undeniably a bit plain to look at, but they taste so good – with hints of ginger and orange and the crunch of fig seeds – that any aesthetic deficiencies are easily forgiven. Have them at teatime or, with cream, for pudding.

Makes 12
125g (4½oz) ground almonds
125g (4½oz) dark brown sugar
generous ½ tsp baking powder
¼ tsp cinnamon
125g (4½oz) ready-to-eat dried figs, stalks removed
2 balls of stem ginger
juice and zest of 1 orange
3 medium eggs

Preheat the oven to 190°C/375°F/Gas Mark 5. Put 6cm (2½in) paper cupcake cases into a 12-hole tartlet or muffin tin (I prefer the latter, as it gives the cakes a square edge rather than a sloping one).

Mix together the almonds, sugar, baking powder and cinnamon until well combined. Whizz the figs in a food processor or blender with the ginger, orange juice and zest for a few seconds until blitzed to a paste.

Combine the fig gloop with the almond mixture, then thoroughly beat in the eggs, one at a time, until you have a smooth batter.

Divide the mixture evenly between the cupcake cases and smooth the tops. Bake for 25 minutes, turning the tray halfway through. Remove from the oven, take the cakes (in their cases) out of the tin and leave to cool. Eat just as they are, or with cream or vanilla ice cream.

Baked figs with chocolate sauce and ice cream

Figs turn a childish pudding into something rather more grown up. The contrast between the slightly leafy flavour of the fruit and the cocoa depth of the chocolate is a particularly good one.

For 4
50g (1¾oz) dark chocolate (60–70% cocoa solids)
100g (3½oz) double cream
scant ¼ tsp ground cinnamon
4 big or 8 small ripe purple figs
a few knobs of butter
vanilla ice cream, bought or homemade (page 99)
a handful of toasted flaked almonds

Preheat the oven to 180°C/350°F/Gas Mark 4.

Break the chocolate into small pieces and put in a small saucepan with the cream and cinnamon. Heat very gently until the chocolate has melted, then stir together to make a smooth glossy sauce.

Cut the figs in half. Place them on a baking tray and top each one with a tiny knob of butter. Put in the oven and cook for about 10 minutes, or until the butter has melted and the figs have softened slightly.

Divide half the chocolate sauce between four small plates or bowls and put the fig halves on top. Add a blob of vanilla ice cream and dribble more chocolate over the top. Scatter with a few of the almonds and dive in.

There's a game I play with my girlfriend. It's called Name That Fish and involves standing in the queue at our local fishmonger's while I point and she names: 'Orange dots – plaice; black spot, big head – John Dory'. I'm not sure she enjoys it quite as much as I do, but she has recently emerged from 20 years as a vegetarian, and I consider it part of her ongoing education in the ways of the flesh.

Depending on the time of year, the fishmonger's cast of marine characters might include pollack, haddock, sea bass, red mullet, cod, ray, hake, lemon sole, Dover sole, John Dory, brill, sea bream, salmon, megrim, mackerel and a glistening tumble of sardines. It's hard to believe that, around the world, fish is in perilously short supply. But the more you learn about sustainability, the more you realise how complicated it is. Tuna stocks, for instance, are facing oblivion in some areas, but fished sustainably in others.

The choice and quality of fish in Britain has improved since we've had to think more about how it's caught and where it comes from. Selling industrial quantities of cod was just too easy. Nowadays, it's not unusual to find fish like dab and gurnard, which used to be thrown back dead into the sea. We're being encouraged to eat more widely, and that's not only a good thing for fish stocks – it's a good thing for us.

If you're worried about what's right and what's not, the Marine Conservation Society has useful lists of fish to eat and avoid on its website: fishonline.org

Baked sea bass
with saffron potatoes

Sea bass
with roasted
peppers and basil

Grilled red mullet
with tomatoes and
preserved lemon

Ray wing
with anchovy
and rosemary

Cod with lentils,
rocket and
salsa verde

Whole grilled
sole with capers
and lemon

Sardines with
caponata and mint

Smoked haddock
with spinach,
mustard and cream

Fish

Baked sea bass with saffron potatoes

Fish roasted in the oven with potatoes is a Mediterranean classic – simple and incredibly good. I've bumped up the traditional flavours with anchovies and saffron. A simple green salad is what's called for on the side.

For 2–4, depending on appetite
2 sea bass (about 450g/1lb each), cleaned and scaled
salt and pepper
a few sprigs of rosemary
juice and zest of 1 lemon
750g (1lb 10oz) potatoes, peeled and sliced no more than 5mm (¼in) thick
4 garlic cloves, crushed
6 salted anchovy fillets, roughly chopped
a good pinch of saffron threads
4 tbsp olive oil, plus a few splashes extra
12 cherry tomatoes, halved
4 tbsp white wine

Preheat the oven to 220°C/425°F/Gas Mark 7. Slash the fish three times on each side with a sharp knife. Season generously inside and out with salt and pepper. Put 1 rosemary sprig into the cavity of each fish. Put them in a dish, pour over the lemon juice, making sure it gets into all the crevices, then leave to one side.

Toss the potatoes with the garlic, anchovies, saffron and 4 tablespoons olive oil. Find a gratin dish that's large enough to hold both fish, side by side with a bit of room to spare. Rub the inside of the dish with olive oil, then roughly layer the potatoes in it. Scatter the tomatoes over the top, along with another sprig of rosemary. Sprinkle with the wine.

Place in the oven for 35 minutes, or until the potatoes are soft and starting to brown. Put the fish on top, add a splash more olive oil and return to the oven for 20 minutes. The fish should be cooked through to the bone.

Scatter with the grated lemon zest and put the dish in the centre of the table. Lift the seabass fillets off the bone, but let people help themselves to the potatoes.

Sea bass with roasted peppers and basil

A gently aromatic idea for a summer lunchtime. You could happily use sea bream fillets instead, or even John Dory if you're feeling particularly swish. The peppers can be made a day in advance and will be better for it. New or sautéed potatoes would be a good accompaniment.

For 4
4 red peppers
4 yellow peppers
1 garlic clove, peeled and crushed
6 tbsp extra-virgin olive oil, plus a splash or two more
salt and pepper
a squeeze of lemon
2 handfuls basil leaves
4 sea bass fillets, about 150g (5oz) each

Start by roasting the peppers. Heat the grill, then put the peppers underneath and leave them there for 5 minutes, maybe a little longer, until the sides closest to the heat have turned black and blistered. Rotate the peppers on their axis and char the next side. Continue until each side has been blackened.

Put the peppers in a bowl and cover the top with a piece of clingfilm. Leave them there for 15–20 minutes, then slip off the skins. Cut them in half and remove the seeds, along with any pale membrane.

Slice the softened flesh into strips about 1cm (½in) wide and throw into a bowl with the garlic and olive oil. Season well, particularly with salt, and add a squeeze of lemon juice, then shred half the basil and stir it in. You can put it in the fridge at this stage, but bring it back to room temperature before you eat.

Cut each fillet in half diagonally across the middle. Pat dry and season well. Heat 2 tablespoons of oil in a large, hot frying pan. Add the fillets, skin side down, and press down briefly with your fingers to stop them curling. Cook for about 2 minutes, or until the skin has crisped a little, then turn and cook for a minute or so more, or until the fish is just cooked through.

Divide the peppers between 4 plates and balance 2 half fillets on top. Splash some of the oil from the peppers around the outside, then add a scattering of basil and an extra splash of olive oil over the fish. Finish with a sprinkle of black pepper and salt.

Grilled red mullet with tomatoes and preserved lemon

Red mullet are stunning fish, with a vivid contrast between their two-tone pink skin and the white flesh underneath. They're also robust enough to hold their own against some pretty strong Mediterranean flavours. If red mullet proves elusive, you could use sea bream instead; a similar sized fish will cook in roughly the same time. Incidentally, you could cook the fish on a barbie if the sun happens to show its face.

For 4
4 red mullet (350g/12oz each), cleaned and scaled
salt and pepper
4 sprigs of thyme
juice of ½ lemon

For the dressing
1 ping-pong ball-sized preserved lemon
2 big pinches of ground cumin
1 small round shallot (or ¼ small red onion), finely chopped
2 garlic cloves, crushed
150ml (5fl oz) extra-virgin olive oil
3 ripe medium tomatoes, finely chopped
juice of 1–2 lemons
a handful of chopped coriander
salt and pepper

Slash the fish three times on each side with a sharp knife, season inside and out and put a sprig of thyme in each cavity. Squeeze the lemon over the top, rubbing it well into the slashes, then leave to one side for about 30 minutes while you make the sauce. Set the grill to high and let it preheat.

Cut the preserved lemon into quarters, then scoop out and discard the pips and pulp. Chop the peel into tiny pieces and put them in a small saucepan with the cumin, shallot, garlic and oil. Warm through over a gentle heat for a minute or so – you don't want the shallots and garlic to cook, just to infuse the oil. Stir in the tomatoes and remove from the heat. Add the juice of 1 lemon, then mix in the coriander. Taste and season, adding more lemon juice if you think it needs it. Depending on the saltiness of your preserved lemons, you may not need any salt – see what you think.

Rub a couple of metal baking sheets – or the bars of the grill shelf – with oil and arrange the fish on top. Place under the grill and cook for 3–4 minutes each side, or until the skin has crisped and the flesh is cooked through.

Arrange on a serving dish or plates and splash the dressing over the top.

Ray wings with anchovy and rosemary

Rays aren't like other fish. They have 'wings' – super-size fins with a layer of cartilage in the middle, which make up much of their body. Once cooked, the flesh peels off in deliciously satisfyingly strips. Capers are the classic partner, but this mixture of anchovies and rosemary delivers a similar salty savouriness.

One word of caution: some members of the ray family – and all of its cousins, the skates – are over-fished. At the time of writing, spotted, cuckoo and starry ray caught in British waters are the most sustainable options. Once they're skinned, it's almost impossible to know what you're buying, so go to a fishmonger who cares about such things. If in doubt, the sauce is good with any white fish – try it with sole, pollack or a bit of sustainable cod.

For 4
50g (1¾oz) can anchovy fillets in olive oil
1 plump garlic clove, crushed
leaves from 2 sprigs of rosemary (bin the stalks), finely chopped
150g (5½oz) unsalted butter
salt and pepper
4 tbsp plain flour
4 pieces of ray wing (300g/10½oz each)
olive oil
good squeeze of lemon juice

Empty the anchovy fillets and their oil into a small saucepan and stir over a gentle heat for a couple of minutes until the fillets have disintegrated into a paste. Keep the heat low, or the anchovies will burn and turn bitter. Stir in the garlic and rosemary for a few seconds, then tip the whole lot into a small bowl and keep to one side. Throw the butter into the same pan and heat until it's molten and bubbling.

Season the flour well, then dip both sides of the fish into it, shaking to get rid of the excess. Heat a splash of oil in two large non-stick frying pans (or cook the fish in two batches in a single pan, keeping the first lot warm in a low oven). Add the wings and cook for 4 minutes, depending on their thickness, then turn them over and give them another 4 minutes, or until the flesh is just cooked through. As you turn, add a few tablespoons of the melted butter to the pans and spoon it over the fish.

Remove the fish and keep it warm, then add the rest of the melted butter to one of the pans, turn up the heat, and let it bubble away until it froths and foams and it just starts to brown. Quickly stir in the anchovy mixture and add a good squeeze of lemon juice. Pour over the fish and serve.

Cod with lentils, rocket and salsa verde

The combination of flaky white fish and earthy lentils has become something of a modern classic. I first had it, I think, at the London restaurant Zafferano, which was run at the time by the brilliant Giorgio Locatelli.

This is my version. The fish doesn't have to be cod – in fact, given its somewhat precarious status at the moment, you might like to consider other fish instead. This would work with any chunky white fish, such as pollack, coley, whiting or haddock. I think it needs nothing more than a green salad to follow.

For 4
4 thick white fish fillets (about 200g/7oz each), skin on
salt and pepper
olive oil
a couple of knobs of butter
4 big handfuls of rocket leaves
1 quantity of salsa verde (page 255), to serve

For the lentils
250g (9oz) puy lentils
6 tbsp extra-virgin olive oil, plus a few splashes extra
1 onion, finely chopped
2 celery sticks, finely chopped
1 medium carrot, finely chopped
4 garlic cloves, crushed
leaves from 1 sprig of rosemary, finely chopped
2 tbsp tomato purée
1 bay leaf
salt and pepper

Season the flesh of the fish generously with salt and pepper and leave to one side while you cook the lentils.

Rinse the lentils in a sieve under the tap. While they're draining, heat 2 tablespoons of the extra-virgin oil in a saucepan and add the vegetables, garlic and rosemary. Cook over a gentle heat for 5–6 minutes, or until the vegetables have softened, then stir in the tomato purée and cook for a minute more.

cont...

Add the lentils and bay leaf, together with 1.2 litres (2 pints) of water. Bring to the boil, skim off any nasty-looking scum, then simmer for 35–40 minutes, or until the lentils are tender but not mushy.

Drain, keeping the cooking liquid. Scoop out the bay leaf. Stir in the remaining oil, along with 4 tablespoons of the cooking liquid. Season with a good ½ teaspoon salt and a few grindings of pepper, then mix in half the salsa verde. Cover and keep warm while you cook the fish.

Heat a large frying pan. You want it really hot. Add 2 tablespoons of oil, then season the skin of the fillets and lay them into the pan, skin-side down, giving a shake as you do so, to stop them sticking. Turn the heat down a little and leave the fillets to cook for 3–4 minutes, depending on thickness, until the skin has crisped and the flesh is cooked two-thirds of the way through. Carefully turn the fillets over, adding a couple of lumps of butter as you do so. Cook for 1 minute more – 1½ minutes if the fillets are very thick; the fish should be just cooked through – and spoon the melted butter over the top as you go. The flesh should divide easily into flakes when poked with a finger.

Stir the rocket into the lentils and divide between four plates or wide bowls. Top each mound of lentils with one of the fillets. Add a splash more olive oil and a few blobs of the remaining salsa verde.

Whole grilled sole with capers and lemon

This is one of my regular greedy lunches, made with whatever flat fish
I happen to find at the fishmongers. Cooked on the bone and doused in
something buttery, there are few things more delicious. The sauce is a
variation on the classic meunière trinity of butter, parsley and lemon, given
extra punch with a sprinkling of capers. It would work well with some of
the lesser flat fish, such as dab, megrim and witch, which need a little more
encouragement in the flavour department.

The quantities are for two, simply because you can manageably cook only
a couple of sole at a time under the grill.

For 2
4 tbsp butter
2 tbsp plain flour
salt and pepper
2 whole Dover or lemon sole (about 350–450g/12oz–1lb each), cleaned and
  trimmed (ask your fishmonger to remove the top skin and scale the bottom)
1 tbsp small capers, rinsed and drained if salted or with vinegar squeezed out
1 tbsp finely chopped parsley
a couple of good squeezes of lemon, plus a couple of lemon quarters to serve

Preheat the grill on a high setting. Melt the butter in a small saucepan and
use a little of it to brush a shallow metal roasting tray or grill pan – this will
stop the fish from sticking.

Season the flour with some salt and pepper and put it on a wide plate. Dip the
fleshy side of the fish into the flour and shake off any excess. Place them side
by side on the buttered tray, skin-side down, and brush the flesh with some
more of the melted butter.

Slide them under the grill – about 7.5cm (3in) from the heat and with the tails
facing towards you – and leave them there for 4 minutes. Brush with more of
the butter and return to the grill for another 2–3 minutes.

Unless the fish are particularly thick, you shouldn't need to turn them – the
heat from the metal tray should cook the underside. Check they're done by
giving a prod with a small knife; they should be cooked through to the bone.

While the fish is cooking, reheat the butter and let it bubble away until it
starts to turn a pale golden brown – the bubbling will subside dramatically
when it reaches the right point. Remove from the heat, season well, and stir
in the capers, parsley and lemon juice.

Slide the fish onto plates, pour over the flavoured butter and eat with an extra
wedge of lemon for squeezing.

Sardines with caponata and mint

Caponata – a kind of sweet-sour Sicilian ratatouille with raisins, olives and capers – is a particularly good foil to the salty richness of sardines. This needs no other accompaniment than a hunk of bread and a squeeze of lemon.

For 4
8–12 small sprigs of rosemary
8–12 Cornish sardines, depending on size, cleaned and gutted
olive oil
sea salt flakes
2–3 pinches of dried crushed chilli flakes
1 lemon for squeezing

For the caponata
6 tbsp extra-virgin olive oil, plus extra for sprinkling
1 red onion, finely sliced
4 celery sticks, finely sliced
4 garlic cloves, crushed
500g (1lb 2oz) aubergines, cut into 2cm (¾in) chunks
2 tsp ground cumin
a pinch of dried crushed chilli flakes
3 tbsp pine nuts
2 tbsp raisins
3 tbsp capers, rinsed and drained if salted or with vinegar squeezed out
10 Kalamata olives, pitted and halved
4 medium tomatoes, roughly chopped
salt and pepper
1 tbsp caster sugar
3 tbsp red wine vinegar
a big handful of mint leaves, torn, plus a few more for scattering

Heat 2 tablespoons olive oil in a large frying pan and add the onion, celery and garlic. Cook for 6–8 minutes over a medium heat, until the onions are soft and sweet. Remove from the pan and keep to one side.

Turn up the heat a bit, add another 4 tablespoons olive oil and throw in the aubergines. Cook for about 8 minutes, stirring them around frequently so all the aubergine has a chance to soften and brown, then sprinkle in the cumin, chilli, pine nuts, raisins, capers and olives, and fry for a minute or so more. Put the onion and garlic mixture back in the pan and add the tomatoes.

cont…

Season well – you want at least ½ tsp salt – and cook for 10 minutes, stirring occasionally, until the tomatoes have softened. Sprinkle the sugar and 2 tablespoons vinegar over the top and stir together for a minute until well combined. Remove from the heat, then stir in the handful of mint and the remaining vinegar.

Let everything cool to room temperature, then have a taste and add more seasoning, vinegar and sugar as you see fit. It will keep in the fridge for a couple of days, getting better as it does so, but bring it back to room temperature before you serve it.

About 1 hour before you want to eat, put a bit of rosemary in the cavity of each sardine, pushing the stem out through the mouth to keep it in place. Rub a little oil over the skin, sprinkle generously inside and out with sea salt and add a scattering of chilli flakes. Leave to one side.

Preheat a grill – or barbecue – and cook the fish for 2–4 minutes each side, or until the skin is crisp and blistered and the flesh is cooked through to the bone. Serve with a blob of the caponata, sprinkling both with a splash more olive oil and a few more mint leaves, plus a squeeze of lemon if you want it.

Smoked haddock with spinach, mustard and cream

I could eat this rather more often than is entirely healthy. There is much to love about it: the smoky intensity of the fish, the enveloping richness of the mustard cream, the way the whole thing browns and crisps around the edges. Use undyed, naturally smoked fish if you can. The DayGlo yellow stuff doesn't compare. Eat with the simplest of green salads.

For 4
600g (1lb 5oz) undyed smoked haddock fillet, skinned
500g (1lb 2oz) baby spinach leaves
250ml (9fl oz) double cream
1 garlic clove, crushed
2 bay leaves
a squeeze of lemon juice
3 big handfuls of finely grated Parmesan cheese
1 tbsp whole grain mustard
a generous grating of nutmeg
black pepper
2 big handfuls of breadcrumbs
large knob of butter

Preheat the oven to 180°C/350°F/Gas Mark 4.

Boil the kettle and put the fish in a heatproof bowl. Pour the boiling water over the top, gently pushing the fish down so it's completely covered. Leave in the water for 5 minutes, then drain thoroughly.

Rinse the spinach and throw it into a large saucepan. Add a lid and let it bubble away for 3 minutes until it starts to wilt, then uncover the pan and stir over the heat for a few minutes until it has softened. Drain in a colander and leave to cool a little, then squeeze out the liquid with your hands and spread the spinach over the bottom of an ovenproof dish – mine is 23 x 23cm (9 x 9in).

Cut the haddock fillets into 8 equal chunks, removing any bones, and put them on top of the spinach.

Tip the cream into the saucepan you used for the spinach and add the garlic and bay leaves. Bring to a boil, add a squeeze of lemon juice, then stir for 1–2 minutes, or until the cream has thickened. Remove from the heat and stir in the Parmesan, mustard and a good grating of nutmeg. Season with black pepper, then pour the mixture over the fish. Scatter the breadcrumbs over the top and dot with butter.

Bake in the oven for 30–35 minutes, or until the fish is cooked through, the cream is bubbling and the breadcrumbs are golden and starting to catch around the edges. Leave it to cool for a couple of minutes before you eat.

I used to work with a friend who shared my passion for gratins. We wasted several happy hours discussing the joy of hot cream and molten cheese, and even fantasised about co-authoring a book on the subject. It was going to be called 'Burnt Offerings'.

The word gratin has its roots in the French 'gratter' (to scratch), and many people will tell you it relates to the grated cheese that is often scattered on top. I've always thought it has more to do with the crunchy, sticky, semi-burnt bits that are left welded to the sides when the rest of the dish has been devoured. Eating these remnants of delicious crusted brown is the guilty adult equivalent of licking the bowl.

There's more than one way to cook a gratin. The most straightforward involves simply melting cheese over cooked veg; aubergine parmigiana, with its layers of rich tomato sauce and Parmesan, is the classic example. Others, like macaroni or cauliflower cheese – and the splendid Flemish gratin of braised chicory and ham – drape their main ingredient in a comfort blanket of rich cheese sauce.

For me, though, the best of all gratins is the dauphinoise: thinly sliced vegetables and cream cooked to a melting tenderness. It works just as well with autumn squashes and winter roots as it does with potatoes. My parsnip gratin, flavoured with garlic, mustard, Parmesan and thyme, has even persuaded a French friend that parsnips aren't just for animal fodder.

The power of a burnt offering is not to be underestimated.

Gratins

Aubergine, courgette and basil gratin

A summer gratin of the non-creamy variety – something to eat with roast lamb or on its own with a green salad. Personally, I also rather like it cold.

For 4–6
750g (1lb 10oz) aubergines, cut into 1cm (½in) cubes
salt and pepper
250g (9oz) courgettes
extra-virgin olive oil
1 big red onion, peeled and finely sliced
leaves from 4 bushy sprigs of thyme
6 garlic cloves, crushed
4 medium tomatoes, chopped
3 tbsp red wine vinegar
3 big handfuls of basil
50g (1¾oz) Parmesan, grated

Put the aubergine bits in a colander, toss them lightly with a sprinkling of salt and leave for 30 minutes. This isn't essential, but there can be a latent bitterness even in modern aubergines, and salting helps draw out the juices. When they've had their time, rinse them under the tap and pat dry with a bit of kitchen paper.

Slice the courgettes lengthways with a potato peeler into thin ribbons, and toss with a splash of oil and some salt. Keep to one side.

Preheat the oven to 180°C/350°F/Gas Mark 4.

Meanwhile, heat 2 tablespoons extra-virgin olive oil in a large frying pan and add the onion, half the thyme leaves and a pinch of salt. Cook for 5–6 minutes over a medium heat, until soft but not brown. Turn the heat up high, add another 3 tablespoons olive oil to the pan and throw in the aubergines and garlic. Cook, stirring constantly at first, for 8–10 minutes, or until the aubergine is soft and starting to brown. Add the chopped tomatoes and vinegar, stir in and bubble away over a medium heat for 4–5 minutes, until everything is soft, then mix in the torn basil leaves and half the grated Parmesan and cook for another minute or so. Season generously.

Spread the aubergine mixture evenly across the bottom of a gratin dish, 23 x 23cm (9 x 9in). Top with the ribbons of courgette, overlapping them slightly in a single layer, then sprinkle with the remaining Parmesan and thyme. Splash with a few streaks of olive oil. Bake for 40–45 minutes, or until golden brown on top and bubbling at the edges.

Beetroot and potato gratin

A raunchy dauphinoise with earthy flavour and startling colour. It ends up not beetroot purple, as you might expect, but a deep autumnal russet. It's a good thing to go with a ballsy roast, though I'd happily devour it just as it is, with a salad on the side.

For 4
500g (1lb 2oz) beetroot
500g (1lb 2oz) floury potatoes, such as King Edward
300ml (10fl oz) double cream
200ml (7fl oz) whole milk
2 garlic cloves, crushed
6 sprigs of thyme
sea salt and black pepper

Preheat the oven to 180°C/350°F/Gas Mark 4.

Peel the beetroot and potatoes and slice both as thinly as possible – you want them pretty skinny, so they cook evenly. Use the slicing blade of a food processor or a mandolin if you have one, making sure you have enough perfect rounds of beetroot to cover the top.

Mix the cream and milk with the garlic and the leaves from 4 sprigs of thyme. Season well, then put a thin layer of the cream mixture in the bottom of a gratin dish, 23 x 23cm (9 x 9in), and layer the potato and beetroot on top, seasoning each layer well as you go. Finish with a neat layer of overlapping beetroot slices, then pour the remaining cream mixture over the top and press the vegetables down into it with your fingers. Lay the 2 remaining sprigs of thyme on top.

Put in the oven and cook for 1 hour, pushing the top layer under the cream again halfway through. Poke the vegetables with the tip of a knife to check they are soft and give them a little longer if necessary. Remove from the oven, then leave to settle and cool for 10–15 minutes before serving.

Macaroni cheese with bacon and mushrooms

This contains the holy trinity of comfort: cheese, carbs and cream. The mushrooms and bacon are just there for extra oomph.

For 4

250g (9oz) small macaroni
6 rashers of smoked, streaky bacon, sliced across into strips
50g (1¾oz) butter, plus a knob extra
250g (9oz) large chestnut mushrooms, thinly sliced
4 sprigs of thyme, leaves only
1 medium onion, peeled and finely chopped
4 tbsp plain flour
100ml (3½fl oz) dry white wine
400ml (14fl oz) full milk
250ml (9fl oz) double cream
100g (3½oz) Cheddar
50g (1¾oz) Parmesan
a good pinch of cayenne pepper
salt and pepper
2 handfuls of breadcrumbs

Preheat the oven to 180°C/350°F/Gas Mark 4. Cook the macaroni in boiling salted water for the time stated on the packet. It's usually 10–12 minutes. Drain and put in a bowl to one side.

Put the bacon in a saucepan on the hob and fry for 1–2 minutes, or until it starts to give up its fat. Add a knob of butter and, when it melts, stir in the mushrooms and thyme leaves. Cook over a medium heat until soft, then turn the heat up a little and bubble away until the liquid has all but evaporated. Tip into the bowl with the cooked pasta and toss together.

Melt the remaining 50g (1¾oz) butter in the pan and throw in the onion. Stir until everything is coated in the fat, then put on a lid, turn down the heat and leave the onions to soften for about 10 minutes. Give them a stir from time to time.

Remove the lid and add the flour. Cook over a gentle heat, stirring constantly, for 1–2 minutes until the mixture is bubbling, then gradually beat in the wine – preferably with a whisk – to form a thick paste. Cook for a further 2 minutes, then gradually beat in the milk and cream, and simmer for 5–10 minutes until the sauce has thickened. Keep back a small handful of the cheese, then stir the rest into the sauce, along with the cayenne and some seasoning, until everything is melted and smooth.

cont…

Mix the sauce with the cooked pasta, bacon and mushrooms, then tip
the whole lot into a gratin dish, 23 x 23cm (9 x 9in). Sprinkle with some
breadcrumbs and the remaining cheese and put in the oven for about
25 minutes, or until bubbling at the edges and brown on top. Leave to settle
for 5–10 minutes before serving.

Butternut squash gratin

A wonderfully orange gratin that's a good accompaniment to pretty much
any roast. I think it works particularly well with pork.

For 4
1 large butternut squash (900g–1kg, 2lb–2lb 4oz)
150ml (5fl oz) double cream
1 garlic clove
salt and freshly ground pepper
25g (1oz) Parmesan, grated
about ¼ nutmeg, finely grated
a few knobs of butter

Preheat the oven to 180°C/350°F/Gas Mark 4.

Peel the squash with a potato peeler and trim off the ends. Cut the longer,
thinner bit from the more bulbous part of the squash. Slice the long bit
into circles about 5mm (¼in) thick and keep to one side. Cut the bulbous
bit in half lengthways, scoop out the seeds with a spoon, then cut the flesh
into half-moonish chunks.

Put the chunks in a saucepan with 200ml (7fl oz) water and put the rounds
on top. Cover with a lid and bring to the boil, then simmer for 5–10 minutes,
or until all the bits are easily pierced with a knife. Keep the rounds to one
side and drain the liquid from the chunks.

Mash the chunks with 100ml (3½fl oz) of the cream, the garlic, salt and
pepper, half the Parmesan and half the grated nutmeg. Spread this mixture
evenly over the bottom of a gratin dish (mine is 20 x 20cm/8 x 8in), then
cover with the circles of squash and press down lightly. Dot the top with
the butter and sprinkle with the remaining Parmesan, nutmeg and cream.
Season again, then put in the oven and bake for 45 minutes, or until
bubbling and golden.

Cauliflower cheese

This is one of the very best of all comfort foods. On occasion, I have actively sulked on discovering that a pub doesn't have it as an accompaniment to its Sunday roast. Few things are as good as gravy mixed with cauliflower and cheese sauce. I could eat a bowlful of this all on its own – maybe even with a naughty blob of ketchup on the side.

For 4
1 cauliflower, broken into bits
35g (1¼oz) butter
4 tbsp plain flour
300ml (10fl oz) whole milk
1 bay leaf
50g (1¾oz) Parmesan, grated
75g (2¾oz) strong Cheddar, grated
1 tbsp Dijon mustard
5 tbsp double cream
a good grating of nutmeg
salt and pepper
a good pinch of cayenne

Preheat the oven to 180°C/350°F/Gas Mark 4.

Bring a large pan of salted water to the boil, drop in the cauliflower pieces and cook for 6 minutes, or until tender – but not soggy. Tip into a colander and leave to drain well.

Melt the butter in a saucepan, then sprinkle in the flour. Stir together well and cook for a minute or so over a gentle heat until the mixture starts to bubble. Using a hand whisk, beat in half the milk a splash at a time, until it forms a smooth paste with the flour, then pour in the milk in a steadier stream. Throw in the bay leaf, bring the liquid to a boil, then reduce the heat and simmer for 15 minutes, stirring often, until it's thick and smooth.

Mix together the two cheeses and add all but a couple of handfuls to the sauce. Stir in the mustard and cream, then season well with nutmeg, salt and pepper.

Put the cauliflower pieces into a gratin dish and pour the sauce evenly over the top. Scatter with the remaining cheese and a good pinch of cayenne.

Put the dish in the oven and cook for 15–20 minutes, or until the top is bubbling and tinged with gold.

I made my first ice cream when I was 10. My parents had inherited a vintage ice cream churn, which stood, unloved and unused, on a shelf in the back shed. It wasn't exactly user-friendly. The ice cream mixture had to be poured into a metal cylinder, which in turn was packed into a wooden bucket filled with ice and salt. Then, by means of a handle connected to a system of stiff cogs, you turned a paddle inside the container until the liquid was frozen and smooth. It was fiendishly hard work and should have put me off for life. Instead, it sowed the seeds of an ice cream obsession.

You don't, of course, need an ice-cream maker – ancient or modern – to make decent ice cream. A cold freezer and an electric whisk will do the job well (see How to Make Ice Cream without a Machine, page 99). But a bit of mechanical help does make the whole process easier. I used to have a machine with a bowl that needed to be kept chilled in the freezer. It always worked perfectly well, but I found myself increasingly frustrated by the fact that the bowl had to be frozen again before I could make another batch. I mean, what if I wanted to make both strawberry and vanilla?

Eventually, I gave in to temptation and bought the super-deluxe version. It weighs roughly the same as a small car and is too large for any of my kitchen cupboards. But none of that matters. It makes great ice cream and has fulfilled my modest dream of making two tubs for the freezer on a single day.

Ice cream and sorbet

How to make ice cream without a machine

Making ice cream without a machine is known as 'still-freezing'. The result can be a little less smooth, but if you carefully whisk out the ice crystals, it comes pretty close. Ice cream always takes longer to freeze than you think, so factor that in, and turn your freezer up high.

Put a strong metal bowl or container in the freezer to chill. When the ice-cream mixture or sorbet is ready, pour it in, levelling the top if necessary. Cover.

Place it in the coldest part of the freezer (often the freezer floor) or the quick-freeze section, if you have one. Freeze until the outer rim of the mixture has solidified and the centre is still liquid. This takes anything from 1½ hours to 4 hours – boozy sorbets, in particular, can take a while.

Remove and quickly beat to a uniform slush with a hand-held beater or whisk, then return to the freezer.

Beat again after a further 1½–2 hours, refreeze, then beat once more after another 1½–2 hours. For the final beating, use a food processor for the smoothest texture. Return to the freezer to firm up completely.

Vanilla ice cream

This is where it all begins: a creamy, frozen custard, minutely studded with specks of vanilla. I can think of no occasion when it isn't an entirely appropriate pud.

For 4
1 vanilla pod
300ml (10fl oz) whole milk
4 medium egg yolks
125g (4½oz) caster sugar
250ml (9fl oz) whipping cream, chilled

Slit the vanilla pod lengthways and scrape the seeds into a small non-stick saucepan. Throw in the scraped pod, then add the milk and bring to a gentle simmer. Turn off the heat, cover the pan and leave to stand for 45 minutes for the vanilla to give up its flavour.

Meanwhile, beat together the yolks and sugar until they're light and fluffy. Quickly reheat the milk and whisk one-quarter of the liquid into the yolk mixture. Then add the remaining milk and stir in well.

cont…

Clean out the non-stick saucepan (it does need to be non-stick) and tip in the custard mixture. Fill the sink with 2–3cm (¾–1¼in) cold water. Cook the custard over a very gentle heat, stirring constantly, until it thickens enough to coat the back of a wooden spoon. You want, at all costs, to avoid making scrambled egg, so don't be tempted to turn up the heat or the custard will curdle. To check if it has thickened, run a finger through the custard on the back of the spoon: if you leave a clean, unwavering line, it is done.

Give it a stir, then plunge the base of the pan into the water-filled sink. Leave to cool, stirring occasionally, until it reaches room temperature; this will take about 20 minutes. Cover with clingfilm and chill in the fridge.

When the custard is cold, remove the vanilla pod, then strain into the cream and either churn in an ice cream machine or still-freeze (see page 99). Once it's churned, tip into a freezer container and put in the freezer to firm up. If it freezes solid, transfer to the fridge for 20 minutes before serving.

And a few simple pleasures to go with it . . .

Affogato
Pour a shot of strong hot espresso over a couple of balls of vanilla. A grown-up, Italian pick-me-up, with satisfying contrasts of warm and cold, bitter and sweet.

Sweet sherry
Pour a small glassful of the sweetest sherry you can find over the top, preferably Pedro Ximenez, the most syrupy of all sherries, which has a deep richness and dried fruit flavours reminiscent of Christmas pudding. You could soak some raisins in the sherry beforehand and throw them in as well.

Hot chocolate sauce
I adored this as a child. I still do. 'I'd like a vanilla ice cream with hot chocolate sauce' was the first thing I learnt to say in German and about the only thing I still remember. For the chocolate sauce, put 50g (1¾oz) good-quality dark chocolate and 100g (3½oz) double cream in a pan, heat gently without boiling, then whisk until smooth and shiny.

Preserved cherries in alcohol
If you ever come across a jar of morello cherries preserved in booze – sometimes called griottes or griottines – get one for the cupboard. A spoonful with vanilla ice cream is a winning combination.

Amaretto
I'm not quite sure if this is super-trashy or terribly sophisticated, but it's rather good. Pour a slug over the top of your vanilla.

Honey and thyme ice cream

There's just a teasing hint of the herbal here, as if it were made with thyme honey. Don't be tempted to up the number of sprigs too dramatically. Woody herbs make spectacular ice creams – rosemary, bay and lavender as well as thyme – but you have to go carefully, or you end up with something that tastes like frozen bubble bath.

For 4
300ml (10fl oz) whole milk
15 single sprigs of fresh thyme
1 strip lemon peel, about 10cm (4in) long and 1cm (½in) wide
4 egg yolks
150ml (5fl oz) runny honey
¼ tsp natural vanilla extract
250ml (9fl oz) whipping cream, chilled

Put the milk in a small non-stick saucepan, along with the thyme and lemon. Bring to a gentle simmer, then turn off the heat, cover the pan and leave the milk to infuse for 45 minutes.

In a heatproof bowl, beat together the egg yolks and honey with a splash of vanilla extract. Reheat the milk to a simmer again, then whisk a third into the beaten egg mixture. When everything is combined, tip the liquid back into the pan with the remaining milk. Stir over a gentle heat to make a custard (for instructions, see recipe for Vanilla Ice Cream on page 99), then quickly cool and chill in the fridge. Strain the cool liquid into the cream, leaving behind the thyme and lemon, then churn in an ice cream maker or still-freeze.

Seville orange ice cream

A recipe for January, when the sharp, pippy marmalade oranges briefly arrive from Spain. They make a particularly zesty ice cream. At other times of year, you can make a fair approximation of both the zest and juice by mixing equal quantities of orange and lime or lemon.

For 4
4 Seville oranges
4 medium egg yolks
175g (6oz) caster sugar
200ml (7fl oz) whole milk
250ml (9fl oz) whipping cream, chilled

cont...

Finely grate the zest of all the oranges, then squeeze 2 of them. Measure out 50ml (2fl oz) of the juice into a heatproof bowl and whisk with the egg yolks, sugar and half the zest, until the mixture is frothy.

Put the milk in a non-stick saucepan and bring to a simmer, then quickly beat a third of it into the egg mixture. Tip the whole lot back into the milk pan. Stir over a gentle heat to make a custard (for instructions, see recipe for Vanilla Ice Cream on page 99), then quickly cool and chill in the fridge. Stir in the cream and the remaining zest. Churn in an ice cream maker – stir after churning to mix any zest that might have got caught around the spool – or still-freeze.

Spiced cherry ice cream

I'm not sure why, but the spices in this pink-flecked ice cream somehow make the cherries taste more cherryish. You might like to serve this with some amaretti biscuits.

For 4
400g (14oz) cherries, pitted
1 whole star anise
¼ tsp ground cinnamon
juice of 1 lemon
2 tbsp caster sugar
4 egg yolks
100g (3½oz) caster sugar
¼ tsp natural vanilla extract
300ml (10fl oz) whole milk
250ml (9fl oz) whipping cream, chilled

Put the cherries in a saucepan with the star anise, cinnamon, lemon and 2 tablespoons sugar. Bring to a simmer and cook over a gentle heat for 10–15 minutes, or until the fruit is soft. Remove the star anise, then blitz the cherries to a purée in a blender or food processor. Leave to cool, then put in the fridge to chill.

In a heatproof bowl, whisk together the egg yolks, sugar and vanilla. Heat the milk to a simmer and use to make a custard with the egg mixture (for instructions, see recipe for Vanilla Ice Cream on page 99), then quickly cool and chill in the fridge. Mix with the cherry purée and the cream, then churn in an ice cream machine or still-freeze.

Strawberry ice cream

I'm rather proud of my strawberry ice cream, which I think has a more natural berry flavour than many. For some reason, strawberries have a tendency to taste artificial. Obviously, the more flavourful your strawberries, the better the result will be.

This is the simplest kind of ice cream you can make and involves simply folding fruit purée into a whipped cream. It's best eaten the day it's made. The same method works with most soft fruit purées, though you might have to adjust the amount of sugar according to their tartness.

For 6
350g (12oz) ripe strawberries
juice of 1 lemon
juice of ½ orange
¼ tsp natural vanilla extract
125g (4½oz) caster sugar
300ml (10fl oz) whipping cream, chilled

Cut out the stalks and leaves from the strawberries. Whizz the fruit to a purée in a food processor or blender, then mix with the lemon and orange juice, vanilla extract and sugar. Leave to stand for 1–2 hours, or until the sugar has dissolved.

Whip the cream until it forms soft, lolloping peaks. Stir in the strawberry purée and gently whip to combine. Churn in an ice cream machine or still-freeze.

After churning, scrape into a container, cover and give it a couple of hours in the freezer to harden to a softly scoopable consistency, then eat immediately. If it freezes solid, soften for 15–20 minutes in the fridge before serving.

Gin and elderflower sorbet

This is a refreshing and subversively grown-up sorbet that tastes like a mildly boozy afternoon in early summer. Use one of the strong cordial brands that needs diluting about 10 or 12 to 1.

For 4
175ml (6fl oz) undiluted elderflower cordial
60g (2¼oz) caster sugar
juice of ½ lemon
5 tbsp decent gin, plus a splash extra, if you fancy it
425ml (15fl oz) chilled sparkling water
1 egg white, lightly beaten

cont…

Put the cordial and sugar in a small saucepan. Stir over a gentle heat until just dissolved. Add the lemon juice and 5 tablespoons gin and put in the fridge to chill.

When it's cold, stir in the sparkling water and churn in an ice cream machine. Add the egg white when the mixture is slushy, then churn until firm. Scrape into a plastic container and put in the freezer to firm up for at least 3 hours before serving. Alternatively, still-freeze the mixture (page 99), beating in the egg white thoroughly when you whisk the sorbet for the final time.

The booze in the mixture means it should be scoopable straight from the freezer, but it also means it melts rather quickly, so don't hang around. I like to scoop mine into a small glass and add the merest splash of extra gin. I'll leave that bit up to you – though you might like to put the gin bottle on the table just in case.

Raspberry and basil sorbet

The basil isn't a sledge-hammer flavour here. It floats in the background, adding just a hint of perfume.

For 4–6
200g (7oz) caster sugar
¼ tsp natural vanilla extract
40 large basil leaves
500g (1lb 2oz) raspberries
juice of 1 lemon

Put the sugar and vanilla in a large mixing bowl with half the basil leaves. Pour over 200ml (7fl oz) boiling water, and stir until the sugar dissolves, then leave to stand for 10 minutes.

Put the raspberries in a blender or food processor with the lemon juice. Measure out 300ml (10fl oz) of the sugar syrup and strain onto the raspberries. Blend to a pulp, then sieve well, until only the seeds are left in the sieve; remember to scrape any purée from the underside.

Chill well in the fridge, then churn in an ice cream maker or still-freeze (see page 99). When the sorbet is nearly firm, chop the remaining basil leaves into the smallest possible pieces (you want them to be the merest flecks), discarding any stalks and ribs, then stir in until well distributed.

After churning, scrape into a container, cover and place in the freezer for 1–2 hours until it reaches a scoopable consistency. If frozen solid, transfer to the fridge for about 15 minutes before serving.

After university, I shared a flat with two friends in Notting Hill. I've been downwardly mobile ever since. The kitchen was tiny and designed more for reheating than actual cooking, but on Saturday afternoons, we'd buy a couple of nets of mussels from the fish stall at Portobello Market, where they were knocking them out cheap. Next day's lunch was a giant pot of moules marinière, which we devoured with gluttonous appetites and rather too much plonk. When the slate-blue shells were empty, we'd soak up the wine-rich juices with chips from the local chippie. A bowl of mussels is still one of my favourite lunches.

Seafood has flavours and textures that you simply don't find elsewhere: the sweet plumpness of scallops; the rock-pool brininess of oysters; the softly resistant bite of squid. But they're also the sort of thing that people fret about. Should the shells be open or shut? Which bits can you eat? And isn't there something about an R in the month?

There's really only one rule that matters: seafood must be absolutely fresh. That means finding a decent fishmonger. I've given a few pointers about how to prepare mussels and oysters. As for the rest, your fishmonger will do the tricky bits for you if you ask.

Curried mussels

Mussels with
leeks, bacon
and tarragon

A big plate
of fried squid
with tzatziki

Chickpeas
with squid
and coriander

Scallops with
pancetta, spinach
and thyme

Scallop ceviche

Oysters and some
good things to
put on them

Mussels, squid and other creatures

Curried mussels

Mussels and curry are a winning partnership. This is a splasher and stainer of a dish, so you are entirely justified in tucking a napkin into the top of your shirt as you eat. You used to be able to get special clips – often shaped like a scallop shell – to keep your napkin in place. A dapper friend of mine tried to start a revival a few years back. Sadly, it never caught on.

For 4 as a first course or 2 as a main
2 big knobs of butter
1 medium onion, thinly sliced
1 garlic clove, finely chopped
1 big bay leaf
a pinch of saffron threads
1 tbsp mild curry powder
1kg (2lb 4oz) mussels, debearded and scrubbed (see below)
125ml (4fl oz) dry white wine
100ml (3½fl oz) double cream
a squeeze of lemon juice
a handful of finely chopped parsley leaves

Melt the butter in a large saucepan. Add the onion, garlic and bay leaf, cover with a lid, then cook over a low heat, for 5 minutes, or until the onion is soft but not coloured. Add the saffron and curry powder and stir for a couple of minutes. Stir in the cleaned mussels, then add the wine and turn up the heat. Cover the pan and cook for 5 minutes until all the mussels have opened – bin any that haven't.

Over a bowl, strain the mussels through a colander or sieve. Tip the juices back into the pan and bubble away for a minute or two to thicken them slightly. Pour in the cream and bubble for a minute or so more, then add a squeeze of lemon juice. Tip the mussels back into the pan and stir through to warm things up again. Ladle the mussels and juices into bowls and scatter a bit of parsley over the top.

Storing and preparing mussels
If you're not going to eat uncooked mussels straight away, wrap them in damp newspaper and keep in a bowl in the fridge. They should last for 24 hours.

Live mussels should close when shaken in a colander. Bin any that remain open; they are likely to be past their best. The same goes for broken shells.

Before cooking, the shells need to be scrubbed clean in cold water and de-bearded: grip any straggly threads emerging from between the shells and pull them off. You may need to scrape off the odd barnacle with a solid knife.

Mussels with leeks, bacon and tarragon

This is a variation on a moules marinière theme. Make sure the leeks are totally soft before you add the shellfish. Few things are as disappointing as an accidentally crunchy leek.

For 4 as a first course, 2 as a main course
4 rashers streaky bacon, sliced into 5mm (¼in) strips
a couple of good knobs of butter
1 medium leek, white and pale green only, sliced
2 garlic cloves
2 bushy sprigs of thyme
125ml (4fl oz) dry white wine or dry cider
1kg (2lb 4oz) mussels, debearded and scrubbed (see page 108)
freshly ground black pepper
a handful of fresh tarragon leaves, chopped
5 tbsp double cream, if you like

In a large saucepan, fry the bacon with a knob of butter for a minute or two, then add the remaining butter and turn the heat down low. Stir in the leek, garlic and thyme, cover with a lid, and sweat gently for 5–6 minutes, or until softened but not brown.

Add the wine and mussels, season with pepper, then cover and turn up the heat. Give the pan a vigorous shake, then cook for 5 minutes, or until the mussels have opened. Throw away any that don't.

You now have a choice:
- stir in the tarragon, then serve immediately, ladling the shells and juices into bowl;
- or strain out the mussels with a slotted spoon and bubble the juices for a minute or two to thicken slightly, then add the cream and bubble for 1 minute more. Tip the mussels back in, along with the tarragon, and stir until everything is warmed through and coated in the sauce.

A big plate of fried squid with tzatziki

An amalgam of two Greek holiday specials, this makes a gluttonous plateful for two to share. You might, incidentally, like to try tzatziki as an alternative accompaniment to the lamb cutlets (page 46).

For 2
60g (2¼oz) plain flour
salt and pepper
1 tbsp olive oil
125ml (4fl oz) sparkling water
1 egg white
400g (14oz) cleaned squid
vegetable oil, for frying
lemon quarters, for squeezing

For the tzatziki:
¼ large cucumber (one about the length of your forearm)
175ml (6fl oz) Greek yoghurt
1 garlic clove, crushed
a small handful mint leaves, torn
2 tbsp olive oil
sea salt and pepper

To make the batter, beat together the flour, seasoning, oil and water, then leave to rest for 1 hour. Whisk the egg white to soft peaks and fold in just before cooking.

Make the tzatziki: grate the cucumber into a colander and add a sprinkling of salt. Stir everything together and leave to stand for 20 minutes or so. The cucumber will get soggy and wet. Squeeze out the liquid using your hands and put the drained cucumber into a bowl with the yoghurt, garlic, mint and olive oil. Season and stir together.

Cut the bodies of the squid into rings about 1cm (½in) thick and separate the tentacles into 2–3 pieces.

Heat a 2cm (¾in) depth of oil in a large frying pan – you want it hot enough that a cube of bread browns in about 30 seconds – then dip batches of squid into the batter, letting the extra drain off. Scatter it into the pan, cooking each lot for 2–2½ minutes – try a bit – and turning the pieces over halfway through if the oil is a little shallow. Drain on kitchen roll and keep warm in the oven if necessary. Salt generously with some sea salt flakes.

Squeeze over bits of lemon at the table. I tend to dip the bits of squid into the tzatziki with my fingers, though I'm not necessarily recommending you stoop to my slovenly level. I'll leave the precise degree of table decorum up to you.

Chickpeas with squid and coriander

This was inspired by a bowl of chickpeas eaten at a lunchtime food stall in the Boqueria market in Barcelona. Their chickpeas were actually entirely different and no squid was involved, but I got home with a strange hunger for them and made this.

For 2–4
4 garlic cloves, crushed
5 tbsp good olive oil
zest and juice of 1 lemon, plus extra to serve
1 bay leaf
salt and pepper
400g (14oz) can chickpeas, drained and rinsed
3 big pinches of crushed chilli flakes
250g (9oz) cleaned squid, rings and tentacles
3 big handfuls of chopped coriander leaves

Put half the crushed garlic in a small saucepan with 2 tablespoons olive oil, the zest of the lemon, the bay leaf and a good sprinkling of salt and pepper. Add the chickpeas, stir everything together and cook over a gentle heat for about 5 minutes so the flavours mingle and the chickpeas warm through.

In a large frying pan, heat another 2 tablespoons oil. Throw in the remaining garlic, plus the chilli flakes and stir for 30 seconds, until starting to sizzle. Throw in the squid and stir over a highish heat for about 2 minutes, until the squid rings have turned an opaque porcelain white. Don't overdo it: squid quickly turn from toothsome to rubbery, so nibble a bit after a minute and see what you think.

Add the chickpeas, the lemon juice and coriander and stir everything together. Season again, being generous with the salt, and pile into bowls. Splash with the remaining oil, and dive in, armed with extra lemon for squeezing if you want it.

Scallops with pancetta, spinach and thyme

There are cleverer ways to prepare scallops, but I think tossing them in a pan with something porky remains one of the best. This is pretty rough-hewn and rustic, though it has a generous heart.

For 4 as a snack, 2 as a light lunch
400g (14oz) scallops, with or without their orange corals
3 tbsp olive oil
75g (2¾oz) pancetta, cut into small cubes or 4 rashers of smoked streaky
  bacon in thin strips
1 garlic clove, crushed
leaves from 3 bushy sprigs of thyme
salt and pepper
4 big handfuls of baby spinach leaves
juice of ½ lemon, plus lemon quarters for squeezing

Quickly rinse the scallops and pat them dry, then trim off and discard the raised rectangular bits on the side – these are the muscles that attach them to their shells, and they toughen when cooked.

Heat 1 tablespoon olive oil in a large frying pan and add the pancetta. Cook for a couple of minutes over a medium heat until it's turning golden, then add the garlic and thyme and stir for a few seconds more. Tip onto a plate and keep to one side.

Turn up the heat and add another 2 tablespoons olive oil to the pan. Season the scallops and add them to the hot oil, in two batches if necessary – you don't want to crowd the pan, or they will steam rather than fry. Leave them, without turning, for 1 minute – or 1½ minutes if they're particularly large – until the underside has browned, then turn and cook for 1 minute more.

Tip the pancetta, thyme and garlic back into to the pan. Add the spinach and stir through for a few seconds, until the first leaves start to wilt, then squeeze over some of the lemon juice – you may not need all of it – and remove from the heat. Season with pepper and tip messily onto small plates, or eat straight from the pan, with a bit of bread and extra lemon for squeezing.

Scallop ceviche

I had my first ceviche in Mexico. It was made of conch – a shellfish I had previously only seen used as a musical instrument in Hollywood epics. The bright flavour was a revelation, the thin slices of fish 'cooked' by their sharp marinade of citrus juice, chilli and salt. I've loved it ever since. This makes four small glassfuls, to be eaten as an invigorating seaside blast at the beginning of a meal. Needless to say, the scallops should be spankingly fresh.

For 4
¼ cucumber, peeled
4 tbsp finely chopped red onion
1 medium red chilli, deseeded, cut into tiny pieces
6 tbsp lemon juice
1 tsp sea salt flakes
black pepper
300g (10½oz) very fresh scallops – the white part only
a handful of coriander leaves, finely chopped
2 tbsp extra-virgin olive oil

Cut the cucumber in half and scrape out the seeds. Cut the flesh into cubes about 5mm (¼in) across, then throw them into a mixing bowl with the red onion and chilli. Mix the lemon juice with the salt, and add a few grinds of pepper.

Rinse the scallops and pat dry, then trim off and discard the square of raised muscle on the side. Cut the nuggets of white flesh into cubes of a similar size to the cucumber and add to the mixing bowl, along with the lemon juice and coriander leaves. Add a splash or two of olive oil and toss everything together. Leave to stand for 5 minutes, then pile into small glasses. Provide teaspoons.

Oysters and some good things to put on them

An oyster eaten in winter is like swimming open-mouthed through pristine seas, all cold brininess and complex minerality. If you happen to find yourself with a dozen round-shelled native oysters (in season from autumn through to spring, hence the rule about eating 'only when there's an R in the month'), I'd advise you to eat them just as they are with, at a push, a squeeze of lemon.

I'm less of a purist, though, when it comes to rock (or Pacific) oysters, which are available all year round. Shallot vinegar is the classic accompaniment, but a fragrant, salty chilli and lime dressing – one of my few excursions into overtly Asian flavours – also works extremely well.

Each sauce will dress at least 2 dozen oysters
oysters, shucked (see opposite) – as many as you want

Shallot vinegar
2 small shallots, peeled and very finely chopped
5 tbsp red wine vinegar
½ tsp caster sugar
black pepper

Mix together the shallots and vinegar, adding the sugar and a grind of black pepper. Let them become acquainted for an hour before serving.

Chilli, lime and coriander dressing
1 medium red chilli
2 tsp caster sugar
4 tbsp lime juice (from about 2 limes)
2 tbsp fish sauce (nam pla or nuoc nam)
1 tbsp finely chopped coriander leaves

Cut the chilli in half lengthways and cut out the seeds and the surrounding mebranes. Slit each half a couple of times lengthways, then slice across into tiny red squares. Mix with the other ingredients and leave for an hour before you use it.

How to shuck an oyster

You'll need an extremely solid, stubby bladed knife – preferably an oyster knife.

Hold the knife in your strongest hand and wrap the other hand in a tea towel to protect it. Pick up an oyster in the towelled hand, with the curved side down and the narrow end towards you.

Insert the oyster knife in the hinge at the narrow end, and wiggle it about a bit from left to right. You will have to press quite hard, but eventually the hinge will give way, allowing you to lift the flat top shell by twisting the knife upward.

Slide the knife along the underside of the flat shell to cut the ligament that connects it to the oyster. Remove the top shell.

Keeping the bottom shell level (you don't want to lose the juices), remove any splinters of shell, then cut underneath the oyster to release it, so the flesh will slide off easily when the shell is tilted.

Arrange the oysters in their half shells on a bed of crushed ice or coarse sea salt.

I recently discovered a new word: drupe. I rather like it. It's the endearingly onomatopoeic name for fruit with a single stone surrounded by a soft globe of flesh – including peaches, nectarines, plums and apricots. The word alone is a reason to love them and few things can compete when it comes to sheer drooling pleasure.

I find peaches particularly sublime, partly for their sweet perfume and the shy blush of their downy cheeks, but most of all for the copious juice, which runs over your chin and down your neck. It's love at first bite.

There are a lot of recipes for grilled and poached peaches out there, but I generally think it's a shame to cook them. If you're not careful, they can end up tasting like they came out of a can. They aren't, though, just for pudding and make a good foil to the likes of mozzarella, air-dried ham and cold chicken. The same goes for their smooth-skinned cousins, the nectarines.

Plums lend themselves better to cooking. Much of the flavour is in the skin and in many varieties has a bitterness that is improved by heat and sugar. As for apricots, we rarely get them properly ripe in this country – they tend to go straight from bullet to blotting paper – and they, too, generally benefit from cooking, baked in a tart, softened in the oven or made into a simple compôte. If you happen to find a perfect one, however, try it with some fresh young goat's cheese – it's one of the most wonderful combinations: sweet, sharp, salty and cool.

Peach, prosciutto
and mozzarella salad

A bowl of
poached plums

Chicken with
nectarines and
watercress

Apricot and
cardamom compôte

Plum and ginger
flapjack crumble

Peaches
and plums

Peach, prosciutto and mozzerella salad

When this is made with milky fresh mozzarella and chin-dribblingly ripe
peaches, it's hard to imagine a more blissful – and blissfully simple –
summer lunch. For the ham, you could use any air-dried ham: prosciutto,
Parma, Serrano or one of the good British equivalents, such as Denhay.

For 4
4 ripe peaches
8 slices of prosciutto or other air-dried ham
2–3 x 125g (4½oz) buffalo mozzarella
sea salt and pepper
a small handful of mint leaves
extra-virgin olive oil

Slice the peaches, removing the stones, and arrange them on a plate. Drape
the ham nonchalantly among the slices, then tear up the mozzarella and
tuck it in. Season, scatter over the mint and splash with olive oil.

A bowl of poached plums

This is a vibrant sci-fi sunset of a pudding, the flavour of the fruit
magnified by sugar and spice. It's simple stuff, yet posh enough for lunch
with friends. Eat it cold with cream, ice cream or yoghurt, or warm with
rice pudding or custard.

For 4
750g (1lb 10oz) plums
100–200g (3½–7oz) caster sugar
1 star anise
1 stick cinnamon
1 vanilla pod, split in half

Slit the plums to the stone down the cleft-like crease in their side, but
without cutting them in half. Put 250ml (9fl oz) water in a saucepan and
add 100g (3½oz) of the sugar, along with the spices and vanilla. Heat gently,
stirring, until the sugar has dissolved. Add the plums and simmer for about
5 minutes until they are soft but not collapsing. Taste one of the plums, and
stir in more sugar as you see fit. Then leave to cool in the poaching liquid.
You can slip off the skins before you eat them if you want, though a bit of
rusticity is never a bad thing.

Chicken with nectarines and watercress

A great mix of bright, summer flavours. The sweet acidity of nectarines
has a curious affinity with both chicken and the peppery spice of watercress
and basil.

For 4
2 plump, skinless chicken breasts
sea salt and pepper
olive oil, for frying
2 tbsp lemon juice
4 tbsp Greek yoghurt
6 tbsp extra-virgin olive oil
3 ripe nectarines
4 handfuls of watercress
a big handful of basil leaves
a handful of flaked almonds, toasted or untoasted

Slice the chicken breasts in half horizontally with a sharp knife, so you're
left with 4 thin 'semi-breasts'. Season well on both sides. Heat a couple
of splashes of olive oil in a large frying pan, then fry the breasts for 2–3
minutes each side until just cooked through. Leave to cool for a few minutes.

Meanwhile, whisk together the lemon juice and Greek yoghurt until they're
smooth and runny, add some seasoning, then slowly whisk in the olive oil.

Cut the nectarines in half and remove the stones. Slice the flesh and arrange
on a big serving plate with the watercress. Tear the chicken into ragged
strips and scatter them among the nectarines. Splash with the dressing, then
tear the basil leaves over the top and scatter with the almonds.

Apricot and cardamom compôte

This is unpretentious and delicious, the cardamom adding a hint of perfumed exoticism. In case you're wondering, I'm counting the apricot as an honorary peach and plum – they're all related.

For 4
10 cardamom pods
500g (1lb 2oz) ripe apricots, stoned and quartered
finely grated zest of 1 lemon
100–150g (3½–5½oz) caster sugar
Greek yoghurt, to serve
unsalted, shelled pistachios, roughly chopped

Crush or slice open the cardamom pods and poke out the black seeds from inside. Put these in a saucepan with the apricots, lemon zest, 100g (3½oz) of the sugar and 125ml (4fl oz) water.

Bring to a boil, then simmer gently for about 15 minutes, stirring often, or until the fruit has softened completely and the juices have bubbled down to a syrup. Add a splash more water if it looks like it might burn. When it's done, taste a bit and stir in as much of the remaining sugar as you think it needs. You may need it all or none of it: it depends on your apricots. You do, though, want to keep a bit of sharpness.

Leave to cool, then serve with bowls of yoghurt, scattering a few pistachios over the top.

You can also, incidentally, make this in winter with dried fruit: bubble up 200g (7oz) organic semi-dried apricots with 75g (2¾oz) sugar and 500ml (18fl oz) water – plus the cardamom and lemon zest – and let everything simmer for about 25 minutes. This is good whizzed to a thick purée.

Plum and ginger flapjack crumble

This isn't strictly a crumble, but it delivers a similar degree of satisfaction. What makes it different is the topping, which hardens into a delicious, softly chewy layer on top of the fruit.

For 6

750g (1lb 10oz) plums, halved, stones removed
2 balls of stem ginger, roughly chopped, plus 2 tbsp of syrup from the jar
¼ tsp ground cinnamon
150g (5½oz) butter, plus a knob extra
175g (6oz) demerara sugar
100g (3½oz) porridge oats
125g (4½oz) self-raising flour
2 tbsp golden syrup
5 tbsp double cream

Put the plums in a saucepan with the ginger and ginger syrup, plus the cinnamon and a knob of butter. Heat gently for a few minutes, until the plums have started to soften.

Preheat the oven to 180°C/350°F/Gas Mark 4. Put the plums in an ovenproof gratin dish (about 23 x 23cm/9 x 9 in and about 5–6cm/2–2½in deep), then sprinkle with 2 tablespoons of the sugar.

In a bowl, mix together the oats, the remaining sugar and the flour. Melt the butter in a saucepan. Now add the golden syrup and cream and mix well. Tip onto the oat mixture and stir together. Spoon on top of the fruit, level out in a thin even layer about 1cm (½in) thick – try not to make it any thicker, or it may not cook through. Put in the oven and bake for 40–45 minutes, or until set and golden brown.

Leave to stand for 10 minutes before eating so the top can set a little (this also prevents you from burning your tongue). Cream or vanilla ice cream are the obvious partners in crime.

There was a book in the early 1980s called 'Real Men Don't Eat Quiche'. I'm not sure anyone remembers what it was actually about, but the reputation of the savoury French tart (as in flan, not floosy) has never really recovered. The book turned quiche lorraine into a byword for unmanliness.

I have to admit that I don't particularly like the Q word – I've always much preferred tart – but the notion of combining a pastry case with a light, savoury custard is a seriously good one, and one that lends itself to endless variation. The classic French filling of streaky bacon has a particular rightness to it, infusing the cream with a delicate smokiness. But there are other intense flavours that work similarly well: sweet, buttery onions and leeks, crab, smoked fish, goat's cheese, roast peppers.

Whatever you put in, there are two things that are guaranteed to let a tart down. The first is a soggy bottom – the pastry shell needs blind baking first or the custard will stop it from turning crisp. The other is a filling that has set into a solid rubber mattress. The secret lies in getting the right balance of egg to cream: use mostly yolks, rather than whole eggs, and the texture will be altogether softer.

The British, of course, have always preferred their pies. I'm not sure why putting pastry or potato on top changes things particularly, but as far as I know nobody has ever questioned their manhood. I've included a couple here, just in case anyone's feeling insecure.

Onion tart
with thyme
and Parmesan

Chicken, leek
and tarragon pie

Pea, asparagus and
Parmesan tart

A good fish pie

Tomato tart
with basil and
goat's cheese

Pies
and
tarts

Onion tart with thyme and Parmesan

This is how all quiche should be: soft and unctuous rather than a wedge of savoury rubber. Some recipes require you to cook the onions until they are brown and caramelised. I prefer this blonder version.

For 6–8

1 quantity plain shortcrust pastry (page 260)
75g (2¾oz) butter
4 medium onions, peeled and thinly sliced
salt and pepper
5 bushy sprigs of thyme
4 tbsp dry white wine
300g (10½oz) double cream
1 whole medium egg and 3 medium egg yolks
25g (1oz) Parmesan

Melt the butter in a large saucepan. Add the sliced onions, a pinch of salt and the leaves from 3 sprigs of thyme. Stir everything together, then cover with a lid and cook over a gentle heat for 45 minutes, or until the onions are soft and squidgy, but not in any way brown. You might want to give them a stir from time to time. Add the wine and bubble away, without a lid, for 10 minutes, or until the liquid has mostly evaporated. Remove from the heat and keep to one side.

On a floured surface, roll out the pastry to about the thickness of a £1 coin. You want it big enough to line a round 23cm (9in), loose-bottomed tart tin, allowing for the depth as well as the width. Carefully roll half the pastry around your rolling pin, then lift it into the tin. Ease it into the base and corners, pressing together any splits and patching any holes with offcuts, then trim it so that it overhangs the top by a finger's width. Prick the bottom all over with a fork, then line the base and sides with a circle of baking parchment and put in the fridge for 30 minutes. Put a flat baking sheet in the oven and preheat it to 190°C/375°F/Gas Mark 5.

Fill the baking parchment liner with ceramic baking beans, uncooked pasta shapes, dried beans or rice. Put the tart tin on the preheated baking sheet in the oven and bake for 10 minutes, or until the sides have set. Remove the parchment and beans, then turn down the oven to 180°C/350°F/Gas Mark 4 and put the tart back in for 10–15 minutes, or until the bottom of the shell feels dry and is the palest golden brown. Remove from the oven and trim the top with a serrated knife. Leave the oven on. In a mixing bowl, beat together the cream, egg and yolks. Keep back about 1 tablespoon of the Parmesan and stir the rest into the cream. Season well, particularly with salt, then stir in the onion mixture until everything is well combined.

cont…

Pour into the tart, smoothing the top, and scatter with the remaining Parmesan and thyme leaves. Put in the oven and bake for 30 minutes, or until the filling is puffed and golden and just set in the middle. Leave to cool in the tin for 15 minutes before carefully unmoulding. Eat while it's still warm.

Chicken, leek and tarragon pie

This is simply one of the most comforting pies there is, a mix of gentle, creamy flavours. Use chicken thighs for the filling if you can, rather than breasts: both the taste and texture will be better.

For 2
5 tbsp dry white wine
200ml (7fl oz) chicken stock
1 bay leaf
1 garlic clove, crushed
2 medium leeks, trimmed of hard green leaves, sliced about 1cm (½in) thick
400g (14oz) boneless, skinless chicken portions (preferably thighs), trimmed of fat
25g (1oz) butter
2 tbsp plain flour
100ml (3½fl oz) double cream
3 big sprigs of tarragon, leaves only
1 tsp Dijon mustard
2 handfuls of grated mature Cheddar (about 25g/1oz in total)
salt and pepper
200g (7oz) decent puff pastry, preferably all-butter
1 egg, beaten

Put the wine and stock in a saucepan with the bay leaf and garlic. Bring to a simmer, add the leeks and place the chicken on top. Return to a simmer, cover and cook for 15 minutes, or until the chicken is cooked. Strain the liquid into a jug and put aside. Remove the leeks and chicken and cool.

Tear the chicken into chunksome bits. Wash the pan. Melt the butter in the pan over a gentle heat. Sprinkle in the flour and stir for 2 minutes until starting to bubble. Remove from the heat and, with a whisk, beat in the cooking liquid a splash at a time, making sure each is incorporated before adding the next. Stir in the cream, return to the heat and simmer for 10–12 minutes, stirring often, until the sauce is thick.

Add the chicken pieces, leeks, tarragon leaves, mustard and Cheddar. Season well and stir, then tip into a pie dish with a rim. (I use one 20 x 15cm/8 x 6in.) Leave to cool.

On a flour-dusted surface, roll out the pastry about 5mm (¼in) thick, and 3cm (1¼in) longer and wider than the pie dish. Cut two 1cm (½in) strips from the length and width of the pastry, wet the rim of the dish with a bit of water and use the pastry strip to edge the top of the dish. Make sure you've still got enough pastry to cover the pie (if not, roll it a tad thinner) and lay it on top. Press gently round the rim and trim any excess. Make a couple of holes in the pastry for steam to escape and flute the edge with a fork or knife. Chill in the fridge for 20 minutes.

Preheat the oven to 200°C/400°F/Gas Mark 6. Brush the top of the pastry with the egg and bake the pie for 20–25 minutes, or until risen and golden.

Pea, asparagus and Parmesan tart

I once made this for a friend who liked it so much they asked if they could have it for pudding as well. It's a lovely thing for early summer, when the peas are sweet and the asparagus explosively fresh.

For 6
1 quantity of plain shortcrust pastry (page 260)
150g (5½oz) slender asparagus
a knob of butter
125g (4½oz) spring onions, thinly sliced
200ml (7fl oz) crème fraîche
1 garlic clove, crushed
25g (1oz) Parmesan
2 medium egg yolks
salt and pepper
100g (3½oz) peas, defrosted if frozen or cooked for 3–4 minutes until tender
   if fresh
a big handful of mint leaves

On a floured surface, roll out the pastry to a circle about the thickness of a £1 coin. It needs to be more than big enough to line a round 23cm (9in), loose-bottomed tart tin (remember to take into account the depth as well as the width). Carefully roll half the pastry around your rolling pin, then lift it into the tart tin. Ease it into the base and corners of the tin, pressing together any splits and patching any holes with offcuts. Trim the rim so it overhangs the top by a finger's width. Prick the bottom all over with a fork, then line the base and sides with a circle of baking parchment and put in the fridge for 30 minutes. Put a flat baking sheet in the oven and preheat it to 190°C/375°F/Gas Mark 5.

cont…

Fill the baking parchment liner with ceramic baking beans, if you have them, or uncooked pasta shapes or rice. Put the tart tin on the preheated baking sheet in the oven and bake for 10 minutes, or until the sides have set. Remove the parchment and beans, carefully moulding any pastry that has slumped back up the sides. It happens sometimes. Turn down the oven to 180°C/350°F/Gas Mark 4 and put the tart back in for 10–15 minutes, or until the shell feels dry on the bottom and is starting to turn pale golden brown. Remove from the oven and trim the top with a sharp serrated knife. Get rid of the trimmings. I often just eat them. Leave the oven on.

Snap off the tough ends of the asparagus. Bring a big pan of water to the boil, then throw in the asparagus and cook for 4–6 minutes, or until just tender. Tip into a colander and run under the cold tap to stop it cooking. Leave to drain.

Melt the knob of butter in a small frying pan, add the onions and cook gently for 5 minutes, or until they soften. Keep to one side.

Mix together the crème fraîche, garlic, Parmesan and egg yolks. Season well and stir in the onions and peas. Keep back 5–6 mint leaves, then tear up the rest and throw those into the mixture, too. Spread evenly over the base of the tart, then top with the asparagus, arranging them in a random but unmistakeably artistic pattern. Press them gently into the top.

Put in the oven and cook for 30 minutes, or until the top has puffed and browned a little. Splash 1 tablespoon or so of extra-virgin oil over the top and leave to cool. Eat while just warm or at room temperature. Scatter with the remaining mint leaves just before you eat.

A good fish pie

I think this has a more deep-pile flavour than your average fish pie, but I've kept the main ingredients simple. Feel free to add as you see fit: a few pieces of salmon fillet, for colour, maybe, or some sliced scallops, to posh it up a bit. I'll leave the divisive issue of hard-boiled egg up to you.

For 6
250ml (9fl oz) fish stock
3 bay leaves
250ml (9fl oz) double cream, plus a splash or two extra
1kg (2lb 4oz) undyed smoked haddock fillet, skin on
100g (3½oz) butter, plus a knob extra
2 medium leeks (the white and pale-green part only), finely sliced
salt and black pepper

4 tbsp plain flour
100ml (3½fl oz) dry white wine
1.25kg (2lb 12oz) floury potatoes
100g (3½oz) Cheddar, grated
200g (7oz) cooked, peeled cold water prawns
2 big handfuls of flat-leaf parsley, chopped

Preheat the oven to 190°C/375°F/Gas Mark 5. Put the stock and bay leaves in a large saucepan with 250ml (9fl oz) cream. Add the haddock and bring to just below the boil, pushing the fish down so it is just covered by the liquid. Reduce the heat and simmer gently for 6 minutes, then remove from the heat and leave to stand for 2 minutes. Strain and reserve the liquid (throw the bay leaves back in until you are ready to make the sauce). When the fish has cooled a little, remove the bones and skin, trying to keep the chunks of flesh as intact as possible. Place in a large gratin dish — about 23 x 23cm (9 x 9in).

Wash the saucepan. Melt half the butter and add the leeks. Stir for a minute until they are well coated, add a pinch of salt, then cover and cook over a gentle heat for 8 minutes, or until the leeks are soft but not brown. Sprinkle in the flour and stir with the leeks for another couple of minutes – the mixture should start to bubble. Turn down the heat and gradually whisk in the wine to give a smooth paste, then cook for another couple of minutes, whisking frequently. Gradually whisk in the liquid used for cooking the fish (minus the bay leaves), then bring to a simmer and cook for 15 minutes, whisking frequently. Taste and season.

Meanwhile, peel the potatoes, chop into quarters and boil until tender (for 15–20 minutes). Drain in a colander, then return to the pan and mash with the remaining butter until smooth. Stir in all but a handful of the Cheddar, season generously, then add a good glug of cream and stir again until you have a spreadable mash.

Add the white sauce to the fish, then, stirring gently, add the prawns and parsley. Season and cover evenly with the mashed potatoes. Make a pattern on top with a knife or fork (this will help it crisp up). Sprinkle with the remaining Cheddar and dot with a bit of butter.

Place in the oven and cook for 45 minutes, or until golden brown on top and bubbling underneath. Allow to stand for 15 minutes, then serve with peas, green beans or a simple green salad.

Tomato tart with basil and goat's cheese

It's a charmingly rustic-looking tart, this: sweet tomatoes layered with soft
onions, herbs and cheese. Some tarts are best made with puff pastry, and this
is one of them.

For 4–6
2 tbsp olive oil, plus more for splashing
2 medium red onions, thinly sliced
2 garlic cloves, crushed
leaves from 4 sprigs of thyme
salt and pepper
350g (12oz) decent puff pastry, preferably all-butter
25g (1oz) Parmesan, grated
150g (5½oz) goat's cheese
2 handfuls of basil leaves, torn
5–6 ripe medium tomatoes, sliced about ¼ cm (⅛in) thick
½ tsp caster sugar

Preheat the oven to 220°C/425°F/Gas Mark 7.

Heat 2 tablespoons oil in a large frying pan. Add the onion, garlic and leaves
from 2 sprigs of thyme, plus a pinch of salt, and cook over a gentle heat for
15 minutes until the onion is soft and sweet.

Roll (or unroll) the pastry to give a 28cm (11in) square. Place it on a large
baking sheet and use the tip of a sharp knife to score a line all the way
around, about 1cm (½in) in from the edge. Don't cut all the way through; it's
just to form a rim for the tart. Prick the centre with a fork. Cook in the oven
for 5–10 minutes, or until it rises and starts to brown.

Remove from the oven and flatten the centre of the pastry with your fingers.
Scatter the Parmesan over the base, then spread the softened onions in a
layer over the top. Break the goat's cheese into small bits and scatter them
evenly over the onions, along with half the basil. Season well, then arrange
the tomato slices on top, overlapping them slightly. Sprinkle with the sugar
and the remaining thyme, and season well, particularly with salt. Add a
splash of olive oil and return to the oven.

Turn the temperature down to 200°C/400°F/Gas Mark 6 and cook for a
further 25–30 minutes, or until the pastry is crisp and golden and the
tomatoes have softened. Remove, add a splash more oil and leave to cool for
15 minutes. Eat warm or at room temperature, scattering the remaining basil
over the top before serving.

We seem to have lost the habit of pudding. There was a time when every meal worth its salt came to a sweet and sticky end. These days, most of us are either too busy or too worried about our waistlines to go the full three courses. Pudding is reserved for high days and holidays, an occasional 'I shouldn't really' indulgence.

It's a pity, because a good pud is one of life's great pleasures. As children, we are programmed to like sweet things and, although our attachment tends to fade as we get older, you only have to watch an octogenarian tucking into treacle sponge or apple crumble to know that it never leaves us completely.

There are recipes for various kinds of pudding here, from calorific old-school favourites to demure little numbers that appear positively restrained in comparison. If you can't find what you're looking for, have a browse through the rest of the book. There are sweet things hidden in other chapters as well.

Banana and black
pepper tarte tatin

Little orange
and lemon pots

Little chocolate pots
with cardamom

Steamed apple
sponge

Linzer torte
cheesecake

Rice pudding with
alcoholic prunes

Pudding

Banana and black pepper tarte tatin

I have a strange and occasional habit of eating mushed bananas on toast with butter, salt and ground pepper. If you haven't tried it, give it a go – it's rather good. So, too, is this take on the same idea, restyled as a tarte tatin. The salted caramel soaks deliciously into the bananas, while the pepper is reborn as a spice, rather than a mere condiment.

For 4
100g (3½oz) caster sugar
50g (1¾oz) butter
sea salt flakes and freshly ground black pepper
3–4 ripe, but not squishy, bananas, peeled and sliced 1cm (½in) thick
1 quantity sweet shortcrust pastry (page 260)

Preheat the oven to 200°C/400°F/Gas Mark 6.

Put the caster sugar in a saucepan with 2 tablespoons water and stir over a gentle heat until the sugar melts and the mixture starts to bubble. Turn up the heat a little, and cook for a further 5–6 minutes, or until it turns to a good caramel colour, swirling the pan gently from time to time to help it brown evenly. Don't let it burn, but do be brave, or it will just taste like melted sugar rather than caramel. When it reaches the right colour, remove it from the heat and add another 1 tablespoon water (the shock will make it splutter and partially reset, then remelt). Throw in the butter in lumps and stir to a smooth sauce.

Mix in 4 pinches of sea salt flakes, then pour into the base of an 18cm (7in) sandwich tin (not a loose-bottomed tin, or the caramel might seep out) and scatter 5 pinches of ground black pepper over the top. Leave to cool for 5 minutes, then add the slices of banana, pressing them into the caramel and pushing them together a little so they fill most of the gaps.

Remove the pastry from the fridge and cut it in half. Put half in the freezer for next time. Roll out the remaining pastry on a well-floured surface to give a circle about the thickness of a £1 coin and about 1cm (½in) wider than your tin. Place the pastry on top of the bananas and tuck it in around the edges, so it forms a sort of shallow upturned bowl over the fruit. Prick the pastry all over with a fork.

Place in the oven and bake for 30 minutes, or until the pastry is cooked through and golden brown. Leave to cool for 10 minutes, then run a knife around the edge, place a large plate over the top and invert the tart onto the plate, repositioning any stray bits of banana. Try to avoid scalding yourself with hot caramel. Serve while just warm, with cream or vanilla ice cream.

Little orange and lemon pots

This is really two recipes in one: a sweet orange compôte and a tart lemon posset. Use crimson-fleshed blood oranges when they are season early in the year. The contrast is particularly dramatic.

For 4
4 oranges or blood oranges
a pinch of ground cinnamon
100g (3½oz) granulated sugar
100ml (3½fl oz) water
150ml (5fl oz) double cream, for whipping

For the posset
450ml (16fl oz) double cream
100g (3½oz) caster sugar
juice and finely grated zest of 2 lemons

Use a lemon zester to cut whispy strips from the peel of one of the oranges (if you haven't got a zester, don't worry: this isn't essential). Cut away the skin and pith from all the oranges and slice the flesh into circles through the middle, getting rid of any stray pips and pith. Put in a bowl with the strips of peel and the cinnamon.

Put the sugar and half the water in a small pan and stir over a medium heat until the sugar dissolves. Leave the pan to simmer, without stirring, until the sugar turns a deep caramel. You may need to swirl it around towards the end if the caramel isn't forming evenly. Remove the pan from the heat and hold it over the sink, then quickly add the remaining water. Be careful: it will splutter. Stir over the heat for a few more seconds to dissolve any lumps of caramel back into the sauce, then pour it over the orange slices and zest and leave to cool.

Now make the posset: put the cream and sugar in a small saucepan with 1 tablespoon of the lemon zest (but not the juice). Stir together well, then heat until it just bubbles and leave to simmer gently for 3 minutes.

While it's cooking, measure out 4 tablespoons of lemon juice. Remove the cream mix from the heat and stir in the juice.

Divide the orange compôte between 4 small glasses and carefully strain the posset on top. Put in the fridge to chill for a couple of hours until cold and set. Whip the extra cream and add a blob to each glass, adding a few extra curls of orange zest if you fancy it.

Little chocolate pots with cardamom

Chocolate pots are one of my regular throw-together puddings. I vary the flavour according to my mood: sometimes with a hint of orange or lemon, sometimes, as here, a bit of spice. Once in the fridge, they set gratifyingly quickly.

For 6
15 cardamom pods
200ml (7fl oz) whole milk
200g (7oz) dark chocolate (60–70% cocoa solids), broken into small pieces
150ml (5fl oz) double cream, plus extra to serve
50g (1¾oz) caster sugar
1 medium egg, beaten

Crush the cardamom pods in a pestle and mortar, or roughly chop, squashing the black seeds inside as you go. Put in a small saucepan with the milk and bring to a simmer, then turn off the heat, cover and leave to stand for 1 hour.

Put the chocolate in a mixing bowl. Add the cream and sugar to the milk and bring to a simmer. Turn off the heat and leave to stand for a minute, then strain through a sieve onto the chocolate. Allow everything to melt for a minute or two, then beat together until smooth and silky. Beat in the egg until everything is well combined.

Divide the mixture between 6 espresso-sized cups or small glasses and put in the fridge to set for a couple of hours.

Add a splash of cream to the top of each one if you feel like it.

Steamed apple sponge

This is an unashamedly old-fashioned school-boy pud – sweet, satisfying and rib-stickingly good. You'll almost undoubtedly want to smother it in either cream or custard.

For 6
125g (4½oz) butter, plus a couple of knobs extra
250g (9oz) Bramley apples, peeled and chopped into small chunks
175g (6oz) dark brown sugar
½ tsp ground cinnamon
zest of ½ lemon
2 medium eggs, beaten
60g (2¼oz) ground almonds
60g (2¼oz) self-raising flour
2–4 tbsp apple juice
Somerset cider brandy, Calvados or brandy (optional)

cont…

Butter a 1-litre (1¾ pint) pudding basin. Preheat the oven to 180°C/350°F/ Gas Mark 4.

Put the apples in a saucepan and add a knob of butter. Stir over a gentle heat until the apple starts to soften around the edges. You want to be left with soft but discernible chunks, rather than mush. Remove from the heat and stir in 4 tablespoons of the sugar. Put half of this mixture in the bottom of the pudding basin. Keep the rest to one side.

Mix the remaining sugar and 125g (4½oz) butter with the cinnamon and lemon zest, then beat until smooth. Add the eggs, a third at a time, beating in each bit thoroughly before you add the next. Fold in the almonds and self-raising flour to give a smooth mixture.

Put half of this mixture on top of the fruit, then add another layer of fruit and top with the remaining sponge mixture. Cover with a piece of foil, tucking it in under the rim of the pudding basin (tie it in place with a bit of string if you want to be safe).

Put the basin in a casserole dish and pour boiling water around the outside so it comes about halfway up the sides. Put the dish in the oven and bake for 1½ hours, removing the foil for the final 30 minutes.

Lift the basin from the casserole dish. Spike the top of the pudding a few times with a skewer and pour over the apple juice, mixing in 1–2 tablespoons cider brandy if you fancy a more grown-up version. Run a knife around the pud and turn it out. Serve with lashings of custard.

Custard
This makes a custard that is silkily pourable rather than gloopily thick.

3 tbsp caster sugar
4 egg yolks
1 vanilla pod, split
150ml (5fl oz) whole milk
150ml (5fl oz) double cream

In a mixing bowl, beat the sugar and yolks until they turn pale. Scrape the seeds from the vanilla pod into a small, non-stick saucepan, throw in the pod, then add the milk and cream. Bring to a simmer, then quickly whisk a third of the hot liquid into the yolk mixture, followed by the remaining milk and cream. Wash out and dry the pan. Tip the egg mixture back into the pan and stir over a gentle heat until thickened enough to coat the back of a wooden spoon. Don't stop stirring for long, or the custard may stick. And don't be tempted to turn up the heat: it needs to be just below simmering point, or it will curdle. To check it has thickened, run a finger through the custard on the back of the spoon; if you leave a clean, unwavering line, it is done.

Linzer torte cheesecake

Linzer torte is quite possibly the world's best jam tart, the pastry made with hazelnuts and spice, and filled with a sweet layer of raspberry goo. This is my heretical cheesecake version.

For 6–8

For the base

75g (6oz) chopped hazelnuts (preferably skin on, but skinned is fine)
140g (5oz) digestive biscuits (about 10)
1 tsp ground cinnamon
4 pinches of ground cloves
3 tbsp caster sugar
75g (6oz) butter, melted

For the filling

600g (1lb 5oz) cream cheese
150g (5½oz) caster sugar
2 tbsp plain flour
1 tsp natural vanilla extract
finely grated zest of 1 orange
2 tbsp lemon juice
2 medium eggs
250ml (9fl oz) soured cream
300g (10½oz) raspberries
icing sugar, for dusting

Preheat the oven to 160°C/325°F/Gas Mark 3. Blitz the hazelnuts to a powder in a food processor, then add the digestives, and quickly whizz for a couple of seconds until reduced to coarse crumbs. Mix with the other base ingredients, then press into the bottom of a 23cm (9in) straight-sided tin with a removable base; you want it about 4cm (1½in) deep. Put in the oven for 10 minutes. Remove and leave to cool. Turn the oven up to 240°C/475°F/Gas Mark 9.

Cut a strip of greaseproof paper 85cm (34in) long and about 6cm (2½in) wide, and use it to make a circular collar around the inside of the tin. (This stops the tin from overflowing if the sides are too shallow, and it makes the cake easier to remove).

Beat together the cream cheese and sugar. When the mixture is smooth, mix in the flour, vanilla, orange zest and lemon juice. Beat in the eggs one at a time, making sure the first is incorporated before adding the next. Finally, mix in 175ml (6fl oz) of the soured cream. Pour the filling on top of the biscuit base, level out, then press half the raspberries into the top and smooth off with a spatula.

cont…

Place in the oven for 10 minutes, then turn down the heat to 110°C/225°F/Gas Mark ¼ and cook for another 25 minutes. Turn off the oven, open the door and leave the cake where it is for 2 hours to cool.

Remove from the oven and allow to cool completely. Spread the top with the remaining soured cream and pile the rest of the berries in the middle. Before serving, sift a couple of pinches of icing sugar over the top.

Rice pudding with alcoholic prunes

Good rice pudding is an easy-access comfort, like a duvet in edible form. Sometimes it needs nothing more than a spoonful of decent jam, but I also rather like it with these boozy prunes, which are a delicious contrast.

For 4

For the prunes
250g (9oz) ready-to-eat prunes
1 Earl Grey teabag
25g (1oz) caster sugar
½ vanilla pod, split (or ¼ tsp natural vanilla extract)
2 strips lemon peel, each about 5cm (2in) long
5 tbsp Armagnac or other brandy

For the pudding
a small knob of butter, plus extra for greasing
100g (3½oz) pudding rice
600ml (1 pint) whole milk
½ vanilla pod, split
60g (2¼oz) caster sugar
300ml (10fl oz) double cream

Put the prunes in a bowl with everything except the Armagnac and pour over 250ml (9fl oz) boiling water. Leave to cool to room temperature, then stir in the booze and put in the fridge to swell for several hours or overnight. Remove the teabag.

Preheat the oven to 150°C/300°F/Gas Mark 2. Butter a 1.5 litre (2¾ pint) gratin dish. Wash the rice. Put the milk in a saucepan and scrape the vanilla seeds into it with the point of a knife. Bring to the boil, then add the rice and sugar.

Simmer for 15 minutes, stirring occasionally to stop it sticking. Stir in the cream and put the whole lot into the gratin dish. Dot with the butter. Bake in the oven for 1 hour, or until the top is just set and browning.

Listening to 'Desert Island Discs' on a Sunday morning, I have often wondered what my luxury would be if I ever had to choose. There are several contenders, all, predictably, food and drink related, including a gin distillery and a field of perpetual tomato plants. The current frontrunner, however, is a lifetime's supply of risotto rice and some good Parmesan to go with it.

I could genuinely eat risotto every day and not get bored. I adore the texture: the way each grain of rice is bathed in an unctuous softness yet still remains distinct. But there's a more pragmatic reason, too: you can make risotto with almost anything. Rice may not have much character of its own, but it's a perfect textural canvas for other flavours. You want seafood? Use seafood. You want vegetables? Use vegetables. You've only got butter and onions? No problem. The ingredients don't even have to be savoury: I've seen risottos made with pears and strawberries.

You may have noticed I've included a kedgeree recipe here. It's not strictly a risotto, I know, but I love it just as much. In any case, it's only another way of adding flavour to rice. The main difference, apart from the rice itself, is how it's cooked. With a pilaf – which is what kedgeree is – you add all the liquid at the beginning and leave things alone. With a risotto, you stir it in a bit at a time, breaking up the starch as you go, so the whole thing turns creamy and smooth.

Risotto

Beetroot risotto with goat's cheese

This combines subtle earthiness with an almost fluorescent colour. The contrast of the beetroot, cheese and chives is particularly exciting.

For 2
1 litre (1¾ pints) vegetable stock
250g (9oz) raw beetroot, peeled and grated
2 tbsp olive oil
½ medium onion, finely chopped
½ stick of celery, finely chopped
1 garlic clove, finely chopped
175g (6oz) risotto rice
100ml (3½fl oz) dry white wine
salt and freshly ground pepper
125g (4½oz) mild, soft, rindless goat's cheese
25g (1oz) butter
a few chopped chives

Put the stock in a saucepan and throw in the beetroot. Bring to a simmer, then reduce the heat and keep it warm; it should be just below simmering point. Meanwhile, in a heavy pan, heat the oil and sweat the onion, garlic and celery over a gentle heat until soft, but not coloured. Add the rice, turn up the heat a little, and stir until well coated in the oil. Throw in the wine and stir until the liquid has been absorbed. Now add 2 ladlefuls of the hot stock, scooping up some of the beetroot bits at the same time, and continue to cook over a medium heat, stirring often, until the liquid is absorbed. Then add another ladle of stock and beetroot, and again stir until absorbed. Season well with salt and pepper, then add a third quantity of stock and stir in. Keep adding stock in this way until the rice grains are just al dente. Use a splash of boiling water if the stock runs out.

Once the rice is cooked, season well, stir in the butter and half the goat's cheese, then cover the pan and leave off the heat for 3 minutes. Taste and season again if you think it needs it.

To serve, spoon the risotto into wide bowls, adding a blob more goat's cheese, and scatter the top with a decorative sprinkle of chopped chives.

Leek and mascarpone risotto

One of the many things I love about risotto is that it takes just a handful of ingredients to concoct something incredibly good. This is one of my favourites and plays on the wonderful affinity between leeks and cream.

For 2
1 litre (1¾ pints) chicken stock
a big knob of butter
2 small leeks, white part only, finely chopped
200g (7oz) risotto rice
125ml (4fl oz) dry white wine
1 generously heaped tbsp mascarpone
a big handful of grated Parmesan, plus extra to serve
salt and pepper

Pour the stock into a saucepan and bring to just below a simmer.

In another largeish saucepan, melt a knob of butter. Add the leeks and sweat over a gentle heat for 5 minutes, or until soft. Stir in the rice, until thoroughly coated in the butter. Turn up the heat a little and tip in the white wine. Bring to a bubble, then stir until most of the liquid has evaporated.

Add a ladleful of the hot stock and cook until it has been absorbed, stirring constantly. Add another ladleful and repeat. Carry on adding stock and stirring until the liquid has thickened and the rice is just al dente. It should be slightly resistant in the middle, but without any hard chalkiness. Don't let it turn into pudding; the consistency should flow like slow-moving lava. Depending on the rice, the heat of the hob and the size of the pan, this should take 17–20 minutes.

When the rice is cooked, stir in the mascarpone and Parmesan. Taste, season, cover, and leave off the heat for 3 minutes. Ladle into wide bowls and add more Parmesan if you fancy it.

Fennel risotto

A beautiful, creamy, white risotto, gently flavoured with the aniseed notes of fennel bulb. A green salad on the side wouldn't go amiss, along with a glass of something dry and white.

For 2
1 litre (1¾ pints) good chicken or vegetable stock
75g (2¾oz) butter
1 bulb fennel (weighing about 350g/12oz), finely chopped, fronds reserved
½ medium onion, finely chopped
175g (6oz) risotto rice
4 tbsp Pernod
25g (1oz) Parmesan, grated
2 tbsp double cream
salt and pepper

Pour the stock into a saucepan and bring to just below a simmer.

In another largeish saucepan, melt 50g (1¾oz) of the butter, then stir in the chopped fennel and onion, and cook over a gentle heat for 5 minutes, or until the vegetables have softened. Add the rice and stir for a couple of minutes until it's starting to get hot.

Turn up the heat a little, pour in the Pernod and bring to a bubble. Stir for about 3 minutes, or until the alcohol has burned off and the liquid has evaporated. Now add 2 ladlefuls of stock and stir in at a gentle simmer. Keep stirring until most of the stock has been absorbed, then add another big ladleful of stock and stir in the same way. Carry on adding stock and stirring until the liquid has thickened and the rice is just al dente. The grains should be slightly resistant in the middle, but without any hard chalkiness. The consistency should be semi-fluid, flowing gently back into position when you push it to one side. Depending on the rice, the heat of the hob and the size of the pan, this should take 17–20 minutes.

When the rice is cooked, add the Parmesan and cream, along with the remaining butter and some salt and pepper. Stir vigorously for a few seconds until the risotto is shiny and unctuous, then cover with a lid and leave to stand off the heat for 3 minutes. Stir again, then pile into wide bowls, scattering the top with a few fennel fronds and a gentle grind of pepper.

Lemon and prawn risotto

This was thrown together as the result of a 'What's in the fridge?' moment. I inadvertently found myself devouring enough for two – always a good sign, I think.

For 2
1 litre (1¾ pints) chicken or vegetable stock
1 tbsp olive oil
25g (1oz) butter
½ medium onion, finely chopped
½ celery stick, finely chopped
1 garlic clove, crushed
175g (6oz) risotto rice
100ml (3½fl oz) dry white wine
finely grated zest of ½ lemon, and a few squeezes of the juice
2 big handfuls of cooked, peeled prawns
2 tbsp double cream
a big handful of basil leaves
salt and pepper

Heat the stock in a small saucepan and keep it warm.

In another, larger pan, heat the oil and half the butter, then add the onion, celery and garlic and cook over a gentle heat for 5–6 minutes, or until soft but not coloured. Add the rice, turn up the heat a little, and stir for a minute or two until well coated in the fat. Pour in the wine and stir again until the liquid has been absorbed.

Next, add 2 ladlefuls of the hot stock and continue to cook over a medium heat, stirring often, until the liquid is absorbed. Add another ladle of stock and again stir until absorbed. Keep adding stock in this way until the rice grains are just al dente and the sauce around them has turned creamy. Use a splash of boiling water if the stock runs out. The end result should flow gently and slowly when you move it around the pan. It generally takes 17–20 minutes to get to this stage, depending on your rice, your pan and your hob.

Once the rice is cooked, season it well, then stir in the lemon zest, prawns, cream and remaining butter. Keep back a few of the basil leaves for decoration and tear the rest into the risotto. Add a couple of squeezes of lemon and stir everything together, then cover with a lid and leave to stand off the heat for 3 minutes. Taste and season again, then ladle into wide bowls. Slice the rest of the basil into fine strips and scatter over the top.

Kale and pancetta risotto

A winter risotto, with a deep savoury richness. The pancetta can be replaced with strips of bacon or lardons.

For 2

200g (7oz) cavolo nero or curly kale
1 litre (1¾ pints) chicken stock
75g (2¾oz) smoked pancetta cubes
50g (1¾oz) butter
1 medium onion, finely chopped
2 garlic cloves, finely chopped
leaves from 1 sprig of rosemary, finely chopped
175g (6oz) risotto rice
100ml (3½fl oz) dry white wine
50g (1¾oz) Parmesan, grated
salt and pepper

Strip the leafy bits of the kale from their woody stems. Discard the stems and finely chop the leaves. Heat the stock in a saucepan, add the kale and simmer for 6–7 minutes until the leaves are tender. Scoop the leaves into a bowl using a slotted spoon and put to one side. Keep the stock hot.

Heat a solid-bottomed saucepan, throw in the pancetta and stir over a medium heat until it releases its fat and starts to brown. Turn the heat down a little and add half the butter, plus the onion, garlic and half the rosemary. Stir together well and cook gently for 5 minutes, or until the onions are soft but not brown.

Now add the rice and stir for a couple of minutes or so until well coated in the fat. Turn up the heat and throw in the wine. Let it bubble away, stirring often, until most of the liquid has gone. Stir in the kale and a ladleful of the hot stock and stir until the stock has been absorbed. Add a second ladle of stock, and again stir until absorbed. Keep adding stock and stirring in this way until the rice grains are just al dente.

Once the rice is cooked, vigorously stir in the remaining butter and the Parmesan. Season well with pepper – depending on the saltiness of your pancetta, cheese and butter, you may not need salt – then cover with a lid and leave to rest off the heat for 3 minutes.

Stir again, then ladle into wide bowls, sprinkling the top with a couple of pinches of the remaining rosemary – you may not need it all.

A kind of kedgeree

I know this isn't a risotto – it's technically a kind of Anglo-Indian pilaf –
but it's part of the same family. In any case, my kedgeree isn't particularly
orthodox, so I have no misgivings about including it here.

For 4
250g (9oz) basmati rice
250ml (9fl oz) whole milk
500g (1lb 2oz) undyed smoked haddock fillet
2 bay leaves
a big knob of butter, plus a few small knobs extra
1 medium onion, finely chopped
2 tsp good mild curry powder
4 cardamom pods, flattened
4 medium eggs
100ml (3½fl oz) double cream
juice of ½ lemon, plus lemon quarters for squeezing at the end
2 handfuls of coriander leaves
salt and pepper

Rinse the rice well in a sieve under the cold tap and leave to drain.

Pour the milk into a small saucepan. Add the fish and 1 bay leaf, then cover,
and bring to a gentle simmer. Poach for 6 minutes, or until the fish is just
done. Remove from the heat and leave to one side.

Melt the butter in a larger saucepan and add the onion. Stir over a gentle heat
for 5 minutes, or until soft, then add the curry powder, cardamom pods and
remaining bay leaf and stir over the heat for a minute or so. Add the rice and
stir until coated in the curry and onion mixture, then strain in the milk, along
with 400ml (14fl oz) water. Put the fish on a plate.

Bring the rice to a gentle simmer, cover with a lid, and cook over the lowest
heat for 12 minutes, or until the rice is cooked and the liquid absorbed.

While it's cooking, clean out the smaller saucepan and fill it with boiling
water. Carefully lower in the eggs, return to the boil and cook for 6 minutes.
Scoop out and plunge into a bowl of cold water for 1 minute to stop them
cooking. Remove and peel carefully – the whites will be set, but the yolks
should still be a bit runny in the middle.

Flake the fish from the bones and skin, leaving it in decent chunks, and stir
into the rice, along with the cream, lemon juice, half the coriander and a
generous sprinkle of salt and pepper. Scoop into bowls, add a small knob more
butter to each one, then cut the eggs in half and place on top. Scatter with
coriander, season again, and serve with extra lemon for squeezing.

A roast is an easy win: you only have to throw a bit of meat in the oven for people to go 'Aaah!'. It's one of those smells, like fresh bread or frying bacon, which connects to our appetite on an emotional level. It taps into our sense of home and our collective nostalgia for a time when all families sat down round a table for Sunday lunch.

Roasts are actually pretty straightforward to cook, doing their own thing in the oven while you get on with the important social business of talking and drinking. The complicated bit is trying to produce five different veg to go with it. Tradition is one thing; a faff is another. I often just do a big bowl of roast potatoes, a green salad and some gravy. It makes the whole thing lighter and much more relaxed. Apart from anything else, lettuce and gravy are utterly delicious together.

On the subject of gravy, I usually just bubble down the juices with some kind of booze and a bit of stock, scraping up the sticky bits of meaty goo from the bottom of the pan. By all means thicken the juices first with a little flour if you want to. Please, though, don't add anything brown from a jar.

Pot-roast chicken
with chicory

A big roast
rib of beef
with cassis gravy

Roast chicken
with its juice
and aïoli

Slow roast lamb
shoulder with garlic,
vermouth and
rosemary

Roast pork
belly with juniper
and apples

Stuffed leg of
lamb with spinach,
feta and olives

Roasts

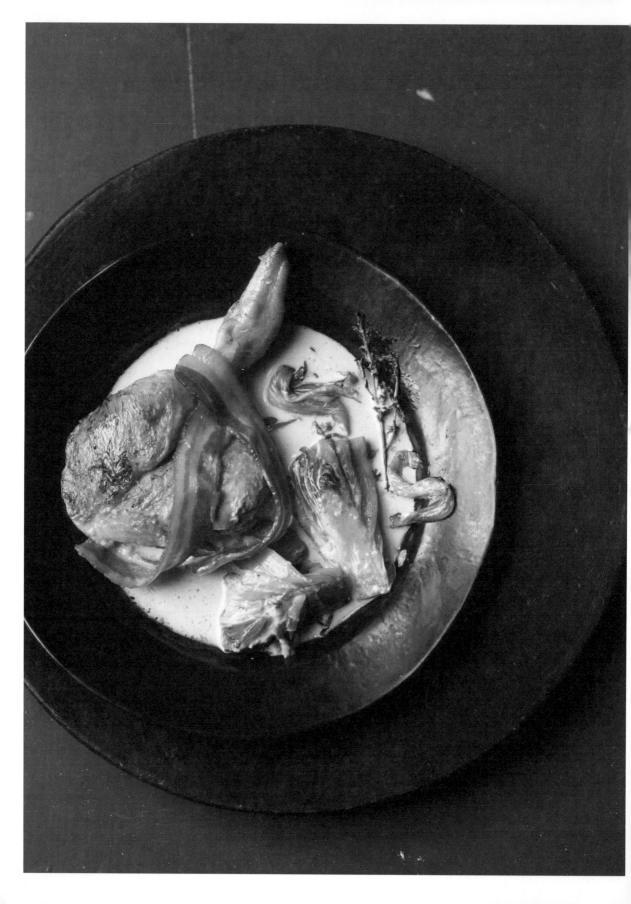

Pot-roast chicken with chicory

This is a great thing to do with a chicken, the wine, cream and juices making a moreish sauce in the pot. It's particularly good with mash. By the way, when I say chicory, I mean what much of the world calls Belgian endive: the tight, flame-shaped bundles of yellow-tipped white leaves. The naming of vegetables can be a bit perverse sometimes.

For 4
1 free-range chicken, about 1.5kg (3lb 5oz)
sea salt and black pepper
½ lemon
2 tbsp vegetable oil
25g (1oz) butter
4 plump heads of chicory, halved lengthways, with the hard cores at the base
  removed
4 tsp sugar
3 plump cloves of garlic, peeled and halved
100ml (3½fl oz) dry white wine
4 twigs of fresh thyme
6 rashers smoked streaky bacon
100ml (3½fl oz) double cream
a handful of chopped parsley, to serve

Preheat the oven to 180C/350F/Gas Mark 4. Season the bird inside and out. Squeeze the ½ lemon and keep the juice to one side. Put the squeezed shell inside the bird.

Heat the oil in an ovenproof casserole dish (you want one with a lid and which will just hold the bird when it is placed on top of the chicory.) Add the chicken and cook over a medium heat until brown all over. Remove and put to one side.

Tip out the oil, then throw in the butter and let it melt. When it starts to froth, add half the chicory, cut side down, and cook over a moderate heat for 2 minutes until it starts to wilt and caramelise. Turn over and give it 2 minutes more, then remove and put to one side. Repeat with the rest of the chicory, then return it all to the pan and throw in the sugar and garlic.

Put the bird on top and add the wine, reserved lemon juice and thyme. Turn up the heat and bubble for 5 minutes, then drape the bacon over the breast. Season, cover and place in the oven for 45 minutes. Remove the lid and return to the oven for a further 30 minutes. Then pour the cream around the outside of the bird and cook for 5 minutes more.

cont...

You can carve at the table, or joint the bird first. To joint it, lift the bird onto a board, pull the legs away and, with a sharp knife, slice through the joint connecting them to the body. Remove the bacon and keep to one side. Cut down on either side of the breast bone to remove a breast and wing, cutting through the joint that attaches the wing to the carcass.

Scoop out the chicory pieces and arrange them on a dish. The juices may have separated a little – it's a rustic sort of dish. If that bothers you (it doesn't bother me), blitz them with a hand-held electric blender for a few seconds. Put the jointed chicken and bits of bacon on top of the chicory, then splash over some of the sauce and scatter with parsley. Tip the rest of the juice into a jug or bowl for people to help themselves.

A big roast rib of beef with cassis gravy

Good beef needs little doing to it, so I've kept things simple here. It just requires Yorkshire pudding, roast potatoes and a dab of horseradish to make it a glorious feast.

For 6
a 2–3 bone rib of beef, about 2.5kg (5½lb), at room temperature
salt and pepper
a few sprigs of thyme
1 onion, peeled and sliced
2 bay leaves
150ml (5fl oz) red wine
5 tbsp crème de cassis
300ml (10fl oz) beef stock

Preheat the oven to 220°C/425°F/Gas Mark 7. Weigh the joint and make a note. Rub the meat all over with salt and pepper, being particularly generous on the fat. Press a few sprigs of thyme over the surface. Lay the onion in the bottom of a large roasting tin, scatter with the bay leaves and 3 extra sprigs of thyme, then put the beef on top so it rests on its bones.

Put the joint in the oven and cook for 20 minutes, then turn down the heat to 160°C/325°F/Gas Mark 3 and give it another 14 minutes per 500g (1lb 2oz) for rare meat or 17 minutes per 500g (1lb 2oz) for medium. The outside will be better done, which is generally no bad thing – there is usually a natural variation in the predilections of the people around the table. Remove the joint from the tin and put it on a big plate. Cover with a loose tent of foil and leave to rest for 30 minutes. There will be enough heat inside to keep it warm.

For the gravy, put the roasting tin on the hob and pour in the wine and cassis, stirring them through the onion debris in the bottom. Let it all bubble for about 5 minutes on a moderately high heat, stirring and scraping to pick up all the meatiness from the tin, then add the stock and bubble for a few minutes more. The gravy will thicken a little as some of the liquid evaporates, but don't expect it to be custard-thick. It's not that kind of gravy. Stir in any resting juices from the meat, season, then pour through a sieve into a jug.

Slice the beef flamboyantly at the table and serve with the gravy.

And some Yorkshire puddings

Your thoughts may well have turned to Yorkshire pudding at this point. I don't blame you. If you've made the batter in advance, individual puddings can cook while the meat is resting.

125g (4½oz) plain flour
salt and pepper
4 medium eggs
200ml (7fl oz) whole milk
4 tbsp dripping, lard, groundnut or sunflower oil

While the beef is cooking, sift the flour into a mixing bowl, season well, then whisk in the eggs. When the flour has been incorporated, gradually whisk in the milk to give a smooth batter. Put the bowl in the fridge to rest until the beef is cooked.

Preheat the oven to 220°C/425°F/Gas Mark 7 (or turn up the oven you cooked the beef in). Divide the fat between the holes of a 12-hole muffin tray and place it in the hot oven for 10 minutes to heat up. Ladle the batter into the holes and quickly return to the oven. Cook for 15–20 minutes until puffed up, set and golden.

Roast chicken with its juice and aïoli

If I had to choose one roast above all others, this would be it. A good roast chicken transcends seasons and occasions. It is what my mind turns to first on Sunday mornings when we have nothing planned for the rest of the day and are free to simply eat, drink and loll.

Cooking the bird on a trivet of vegetables is a good trick, adding sweetness and flavour to the pan. The aïoli is my little foible – I dip the chicken in it and stir it into the juices on my plate.

For 4
1.5kg (3lb 5oz) free-range chicken
1 medium carrot
1 celery stick
½ medium onion
4 garlic cloves, peeled and flattened with the side of a knife
salt and pepper
50g (1¾oz) butter
a few sprigs of thyme, or a sprig of rosemary
½ lemon
150ml (5fl oz) dry white wine
1 quantity of aïoli (page 255)

Untruss the chicken and allow it to come to room temperature. Preheat the oven to 200°C/400°F/Gas Mark 6. Slice the carrot, celery and onion. Place in the centre of a roasting tin, along with 2 of the squashed garlic cloves.

Season the chicken well, inside and out. Put a good knob of butter in the cavity, along with the herbs and the remaining garlic, then smear the rest of the butter over the breast. Place the chicken on top of the vegetables, then squeeze over the lemon and put the shell in the cavity. Pour over the wine. Turn the chicken onto one breast and roast for 25 minutes. Baste with the juices, then turn onto the other breast and roast for 25 minutes. Finally, turn it upright, baste again, and roast for another 25 minutes.

Check it's done by piercing the thickest part of the thigh – the juices should run clear. If there's a trace of bloodiness, give it 5–10 minutes more. Remove from the oven, cover loosely with a tent of foil, and allow to rest for 10–15 minutes before carving. Strain the juices from the pan and the cavity of the chicken, discarding the vegetables, then add to any resting juices. Carve the chicken and spoon over the scant but flavourful sauce. Dollop on aïoli at will.

Slow roast lamb shoulder with garlic, vermouth and rosemary

The lamb here is so meltingly tender that when you come to carve, a spoon does the job of a knife. Roasting garlic with it gives you the makings of a deliciously sludgy sauce.

For 6
2 tbsp olive oil
2.25kg (5lb) shoulder of lamb on the bone
salt and pepper
300ml (10fl oz) dry vermouth or dry white wine
25 garlic cloves, separated but unpeeled
3 sprigs of rosemary
3 bay leaves
a squeeze of lemon juice

Preheat the oven to 160°C/325°F/Gas Mark 3.

Heat the olive oil in a solid roasting tin on the hob over a medium heat. Season the lamb generously all over, then put it in the tin and let it brown for 10–15 minutes, turning occasionally, until the meat is well coloured all over. Remove and keep to one side.

Tip off the oil, then pour in the vermouth and scrape up any flavourful brown bits from the bottom of the tin. Scatter half the garlic cloves and herbs over the bottom of the tin, then place the lamb on top, skin-side up, and strew with the remaining garlic and herbs.

Cover the tin with a double thickness of foil, sealing in the lamb as hermetically as you can. Place the tin in the oven and cook for about 5 hours, carefully peeling back the foil to baste the meat with the cooking juices a couple of times.

When the meat is done, it should be so soft you can almost lift out the bone. Check it after 4½ hours, and be prepared to give it 5½ hours if necessary.

Lift the meat from the tin and keep warm under a loose tent of foil. Tip most of the fat from the pan, leaving behind the dark and savoury juices. Scoop the garlic cloves and herbs into a metal sieve, and use the back of a ladle to push the soft, aromatic flesh from the garlic back into the pan, scraping any pulp from the bottom of the sieve as you go. You should be left with mostly garlic skins in the sieve.

Stir the garlic into the sauce, adding a squeeze of lemon juice to taste, and reheat gently. Serve with generous chunks torn from the shoulder of lamb.

Roast pork belly with juniper and apples

A big piggy roast with sweet meat and crisp crackling. I often throw a bit of fruit around roasting pork: not just apples, but halved pears or quartered quinces. The fruit softens and squidges, flavouring the pan juices as it goes.

For 6
3 plump garlic cloves, crushed
fine salt, sea salt flakes and freshly ground pepper
4 sprigs of rosemary
15 juniper berries
2 tbsp olive oil, plus a splash extra
1.5kg (3lb 5oz) boneless pork belly, skin scored by the butcher
  into 1cm (½in) strips
2 bay leaves
6 small eating apples
3 red onions, peeled and quartered through the root
125ml (4fl oz) dry cider
250ml (9fl oz) chicken stock

In a small bowl, mash the garlic with a pinch of salt. Strip the leaves from 2 of the rosemary sprigs and put on a chopping board. Add the juniper berries and chop both well. Stir the rosemary and juniper into the garlic, then mix in the olive oil.

Place the pork, skin side down, in a large, shallow roasting tin. Poke a few holes in the fleshy side with the point of a knife, being careful not to go right through, then massage the garlic mixture evenly into the meat. Turn skin side up, tucking the bay leaves underneath.

Dry the skin thoroughly with a bit of kitchen paper. If the skin doesn't look properly scored, use a very sharp knife to make a few more slits. Scatter 1 teaspoon fine salt evenly over the skin and massage it lovingly into the crevices. Rub the skin with a splash of olive oil, then scatter over a few pinches of sea salt flakes. Leave at room temperature for about 1 hour.

Preheat the oven to 240°C/475°F/Gas Mark 9. Put in the pork, and cook for 25 minutes, then turn the heat down to 180°C/350°F/Gas Mark 4 and leave it alone for 30 minutes.

Meanwhile, cut a line through the skin around the equator of the apples – this will help them stay roughly in one piece as they bake rather than splitting their sides in a dramatic explosion.

cont…

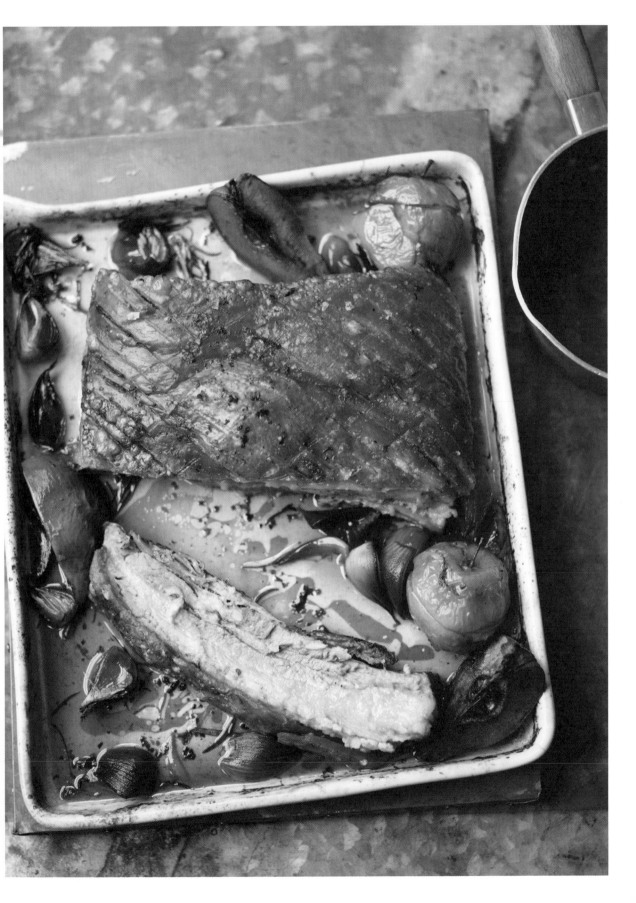

Add to the roasting tin around the pork, together with the onion quarters and remaining rosemary, and quickly toss the fruit and vegetables around so they are coated in the fat. Return the tin to the oven for another 1 hour, by which time the meat should be cooked through, the onions caramelised and soft and the apples on the verge of collapse. The crackling should have popped as well, but if it hasn't quite done its thing, carefully slice it away from the top of the meat and return it on its own to the oven, turning the heat up high, until it bubbles and crisps. Transfer everything else to a serving dish and keep warm for 10 minutes while you make the gravy.

Place the roasting tin on the hob, pour in the cider and allow it to bubble away for a couple of minutes, scraping all the caramelised bits off the bottom. Pour in the stock and bubble for 5 minutes, or until the gravy thickens a little. Taste and season.

Carve the pork at the table, giving everyone an apple and some of the red onion, or just pile everything back into the serving dish and let people help themselves. A jug or bowl for the gravy would be a good idea.

Stuffed leg of lamb with spinach, feta and olives

This delivers deliciously savoury, Greekish flavours. The butcher will have to do a bit of work for you. Ask him to tunnel bone a leg of lamb, leaving the shank bone attached. This gives you a leg with a cave-like hollow in the middle, which you can fill with stuffing. The shank bone stops it all falling out the other end.

For 6

1 x tunnel-boned leg of lamb with the shank bone still attached,
   1.5–2kg (3lb 5oz–4½lb) boned weight
salt and pepper
4 garlic cloves, peeled
12 Kalamata olives, drained and pitted
3 big handfuls of baby spinach leaves
a big handful of mint leaves
a big handful of flat-leaf parsley
leaves from 3 sprigs of thyme
finely grated zest and juice of 1 lemon
3 tbsp olive oil
200g (7oz) feta, roughly broken up
200ml (7fl oz) dry white wine

Preheat the oven to 220°C/425°F/Gas Mark 7. Season the inner fleshy side of the lamb with pepper.

Crush 2 garlic cloves and put them in a food processor with the olives, spinach, mint, parsley and leaves from 2 sprigs of thyme. Grate in the zest of the lemon and add 1 tablespoon olive oil, plus some more pepper, and blitz together into a green paste. Tip into a bowl and add the feta, crumbling it with the herb mixture so you're left with a coarse, chunky paste.

Open up the hole in the leg of lamb and push the feta mixture inside, making sure it gets into the deepest recesses. Knit the lamb together with a skewer or two (or some wooden tooth picks), so the cavity is roughly closed, then put the meat in a roasting tin, turning it over if necessary, so the biggest expanse of fat is facing upwards.

Cut the remaining 2 garlic cloves into slivers. Make 12–15 small incisions in the fat of the lamb with the tip of a sharp knife and push a bit of garlic into each one. Dribble with 2 tablespoons olive oil and rub into the skin. Season well and scatter the remaining thyme over the top. Squeeze over the juice from the lemon.

Roast for 20 minutes, then tip in the wine, scraping any dark juices from the bottom of the pan. Reduce the heat to 180°C/350°F/Gas Mark 4 and return the lamb to the oven for another 1 hour for a 1.5kg (3lb 5oz) joint and 1 hour, 15 minutes for one weighing 2kg (4lb 8oz). When it's done, remove from the oven and leave to rest for 20 minutes, covered by a loose tent of foil.

If the juices have gone cold, reheat them briefly in a small saucepan, tasting and seasoning as you do so. Carve the meat into slices and eat with the juices and the stuffing that spills from the middle.

There are all sorts of conventions surrounding the matching of pasta and sauce. Long, thin pasta needs lubrication to help it slip down, which is why the likes of tagliatelle and linguine are so often paired with olive oil, creamy sauces and meat ragùs. Penne, conchiglie and fusilli, on the other hand, are generally considered better with chunkier meat or vegetables, because their shape scoops up the sauce more easily.

Personally, I've never been that much of a purist. I know it's culturally and culinarily incorrect, and Italians would probably consider me deeply infantile, but spaghetti is the pasta I invariably turn to first. It is my standby for late-night suppers, thrown together with garlic, chilli, parsley, lemon and olive oil, or a robust, savoury sludge of anchovies and capers. In my lazier moments, I sometimes just toss in some salt, pepper and a knob of butter. There's a simple satisfaction to be found in a bowl of buttered pasta.

But don't let my strange proclivities influence you too much – use whatever pasta you happen to have knocking around. The courgette sauce and carbonara, in particular, would go well with penne and the like. The ricotta or meatballs would work with just about anything.

You'll need a big pan and lots of water – 5 litres (about 9 pints) if you're cooking for four. Bring it to a bubbling boil, then add 1 tablespoon salt just before the pasta goes in. Start with the lower end of the suggested cooking time, scoop out a bit of pasta to try, then give it a bit longer if needed. Keep back a cupful of the cooking water when you drain it – it comes in useful if the sauce needs thinning.

Spaghetti with
ricotta and herbs

Spaghetti with
mushrooms
and fennel seeds

Spaghetti with
crab and mint

Spaghetti with
meatballs

Spaghetti with
courgettes, basil
and lemon

Spaghetti carbonara

Spaghetti

Spaghetti with ricotta and herbs

I'm not particularly obsessed with speed in the kitchen – things take as long
as they take – but this is about as quick as spaghetti gets. Once the pasta is
cooked, the whole thing is ready in seconds, the greenery and garlic simply
stirred into the hot pan with the cheese and a glug of oil.

For 4
350g (12oz) spaghetti
4 tbsp extra-virgin olive oil, plus extra to serve
8 tbsp ricotta
about 20 large mint leaves, torn
about 20 large basil leaves, torn
2 garlic cloves, peeled and crushed
sea salt and black pepper
juice and zest of 1 lemon
4 handfuls of rocket
pecorino or Parmesan, grated, to serve

Cook the pasta according to the packet instructions, then drain, leaving a
couple of tablespoons of the cooking liquid in the pan.

Return the pasta to the pan and stir in 4 tablespoons olive oil, then throw in
the ricotta, herbs and garlic, some salt and pepper, the zest of the lemon and
a good squeeze of the juice – you may not need all of it, I'll leave the exact
amount up to you.

Stir everything together until the strands of pasta are coated, then quickly
stir in the rocket and divide among warmed bowls. Scatter the top with the
pecorino or Parmesan and add a sprinkle more olive oil before you eat.

Spaghetti with mushrooms and fennel seeds

Some mushrooms naturally have a faint hint of anise and the fennel seeds coax it out. Add a few wild ones to the mix if you happen to have them.

For 4
125ml olive oil
500g (1lb 2oz) chestnut mushrooms
3 garlic cloves, crushed
3 tsp fennel seeds, crushed
salt and pepper
5 tbsp dry white wine
1 lemon
2 handfuls of chopped flat-leaf parsley
350g (12oz) spaghetti
4 big handfuls of grated Parmesan

Heat half the oil in a large frying pan over a high heat. Add half the mushrooms and garlic, plus 1 teaspoon crushed fennel seeds and a good pinch of salt. Stir over the heat for about 5 minutes. You want the mushrooms to sauté rather than stew. Keep an eye on the heat and turn it down if necessary. Tip into a bowl, leaving most of the oil in the pan, and repeat with the remaining mushrooms and garlic, adding another 1 teaspoon of fennel seeds. Return the first batch to the pan.

Add the wine and bubble for 1 minute more until the liquid has pretty much evaporated, then remove from the heat and add a couple of good squeezes of lemon. Stir in the remaining oil and 4 good pinches of the remaining fennel seeds (you may not need all of it), plus half the parsley and a few grinds of black pepper. It may need more salt, too – see what you think.

Meanwhile, cook the spaghetti according to the packet instructions. Toss together with the mushroom mixture and scoop into bowls. Scatter with some of the remaining parsley, plus a generous handful of grated Parmesan.

Spaghetti with crab and mint

This is a twist on an Italian seaside classic, the sweet crab lifted by the brighter notes of lemon, chilli and herbs. You want about half the crab to be brown meat, so it's a good thing to make with a ready-dressed crab, preferably one without added mayonnaise and breadcrumbs.

For 4

350g (12oz) spaghetti
125ml (4fl oz) extra-virgin olive oil, plus 3 tbsp extra for frying
2 big handfuls of coarse white breadcrumbs
2 garlic cloves, peeled and crushed
2 pinches of crushed chilli flakes
350g (12oz) crab meat (preferably half brown and half white)
sea salt and black pepper
2 handfuls of mint leaves, torn
juice of 1 lemon and the zest of half
4 big handfuls of watercress

Cook the pasta, following the instructions on the packet.

While it's bubbling away, heat 3 tablespoons of olive oil in a frying pan and stir through the breadcrumbs, garlic and chilli over the heat for a couple of minutes until golden brown. Don't let the garlic or crumbs burn. Keep to one side.

Season the crab meat well.

Drain the cooked pasta, then gently stir in the crab, along with half the mint, the lemon juice and zest, and the 125ml (4fl oz) olive oil. Finally, toss through the watercress, pile into bowls and sprinkle with the breadcrumbs and the remaining mint leaves. A glug more oil and a squeeze of lemon at the table wouldn't be a bad idea.

Spaghetti with meatballs

The flavours here aren't terribly Italian – in fact, they're distinctly North African. But spaghetti with meatballs is actually quite a rare thing in Italy – it's the Americans who have made it their own – so I feel no qualms about taking things in my own direction.

For 4
2 tbsp mild (sweet) paprika
1 tbsp ground cumin
¼ tsp cayenne pepper
5 big garlic cloves, crushed
2 handfuls of coriander leaves, chopped
3 big handfuls of flat-leaf parsley, chopped
500g (1lb 2oz) lamb mince
finely grated zest of 1 lemon
salt and pepper
1 medium onion, finely chopped
2 tbsp olive oil
2 x 400g (14oz) cans chopped plum tomatoes
2 tsp sugar
350g (12oz) spaghetti

Mix together the spices, garlic, coriander and 2 handfuls of the parsley (throw them all in a food processor to chop them if it's easier). Mix half into the lamb with the lemon zest and season generously, then massage manfully for a couple of minutes with your hands until everything is thoroughly squidged together. Shape into 24 equal-sized balls, rolling them between your palms.

Heat the oil in a large frying pan and fry the meatballs in 2 batches until just brown on all sides – about 4 minutes for each batch. Remove and keep to one side.

Tip most of the fat from the pan, leaving just 1 tbsp. Add the onion and cook over a gentle heat for 5-6 minutes until soft and golden. Stir in the remaining spice, herb and garlic mix, cook for 1 minute, then add the tomatoes and sugar and season well – you could need up to 1 teaspoon of salt. Stir in 150ml (5fl oz) water, bring to a bubble, and simmer for about 20 minutes, until thick and rich, stirring occasionally to break up the tomatoes. Add the meatballs to the sauce and cover the pan with a lid (or a sheet of foil, tucked in at the edges). Simmer gently for about 10 minutes more. While the meatballs are cooking, put the spaghetti on to boil, following the instructions on the packet. Drain in a colander. Toss the spaghetti with the sauce and scoop into bowls, dividing the meatballs between them. Finely chop the remaining parsley and sprinkle a little over the top.

Spaghetti with courgettes, basil and lemon

There are people who claim not to like courgettes. I'm guessing they were traumatised by mushiness in early life. This fragrant supper could well prove to be the cure.

For 4
3 tbsp olive oil
4 medium courgettes, cut into thin half-moons
4 garlic cloves, finely chopped
a big pinch of cayenne pepper
sea salt and black pepper
350g (12oz) spaghetti
finely grated zest of 1½ lemons and the juice from one
2 generous glugs of double cream
2 big handfuls of basil, plus extra leaves for scattering
2 big handfuls of shaved Parmesan, plus extra for scattering

In a large frying pan, heat the oil over a medium heat. Add the courgettes and garlic, plus a pinch of cayenne and a generous sprinkling of salt. Cook gently for 10 minutes, stirring occasionally, until the courgettes are soft, but not browned.

Meanwhile, put the pasta on to cook – follow the instructions on the packet.

When the courgettes are soft, add the lemon juice, remove from the heat and stir in the zest, cream, torn basil and Parmesan, plus 2–3 tablespoons of cooking water from the pasta to thin the sauce down.

Season generously with pepper, then drain the pasta and combine with the sauce. Toss together, and pile into wide bowls. Serve with a few more basil leaves and extra Parmesan over the top.

Spaghetti carbonara

This will no doubt have Italians tutting in disapproval, so I should point out that I make no claims for its authenticity. For one thing, it has onion in it (tut), not to mention wine and cream (tut, tut). It is, though, utterly delicious.

For 4
2 tbsp olive oil
250g (9oz) smoked pancetta, cut into small cubes, or smoked lardons
1 medium onion, finely chopped
3 garlic cloves, crushed
5 tbsp dry white wine
sea salt
350g (12oz) spaghetti
4 egg yolks
150ml (5fl oz) double cream
100g (3½oz) pecorino, grated
3 tbsp chopped parsley
fresh nutmeg
black pepper

Heat the oil in a large frying pan. Add the pancetta and cook over a medium heat for 5 minutes, or until starting to brown. Turn down the heat to medium-low, add the onion and garlic, and cook gently for 10–12 minutes, or until soft and sweet. Turn up the heat again and throw in the wine. Bubble for 3 minutes, or until only about 1 tablespoon of liquid remains. Turn off the heat.

Bring a large pot of salted water to the boil. Add the spaghetti and cook until al dente (usually about 10 minutes, but follow the instructions on the packet). Drain.

Reheat the pancetta. Put the egg yolks and cream into a mixing bowl and beat together. Add two-thirds of the pecorino cheese, 2 tablespoons chopped parsley, a good grating of nutmeg and lots of black pepper. Mix thoroughly. Add the spaghetti and toss, then add the pancetta and toss again. Taste and adjust the seasoning. Divide between bowls and sprinkle with the remaining pecorino and parsley, plus more nutmeg if you want, then dive in.

'Stews are like bed socks,' my girlfriend announced recently over supper. 'They're sort of comfy cosy.' I'm not sure I would have put it quite like that myself, but I know what she means. Stew is an archetypal winter comfort, on a par with cable-knit jumpers and roaring fires, buttered crumpets and a nice cup of tea. It is food for grey days and stormy nights, when the rain is lashing at the windows and the trees are bending in the wind.

I've always struggled slightly when it comes to defining exactly what makes a stew a stew. If it's just about slow cooking with some kind of liquid, then where does that leave braises and casseroles? And what about fish and vegetable stews, both of which can be made in under half an hour?

I've decided that, in fact, a stew can be pretty much anything hot and savoury, provided it comes in a big pot and ends up chunkier than soup. In any case, what really matters is that it makes you feel warm and happy. And in that respect, it is, indeed, like a pair of bed socks.

Spiced butternut
and chickpea stew

Fish stew
with aïoli

Braised lamb
shanks with
orange

Goulash

Beef stew
with cinnamon
and prunes

Stew

Spiced butternut and chickpea stew

Vegetable stews can be a bit on the watery side, but I think this one, with its different layers of texture and spice, happily competes with anything more meaty.

For 6

1 ping-pong ball-sized preserved lemon
2 tbsp olive oil
1 medium onion, sliced
4 garlic cloves, crushed
2 tsp ground cumin
1 tsp ground coriander
½ tsp ground cinnamon
12 saffron threads
a good pinch of crushed chilli flakes
600g (1lb 5oz) butternut squash, peeled and cut into 2cm (¾in) cubes
2 x 400g (14oz) cans chickpeas, drained and rinsed
1 x 400g (14oz) can chopped plum tomatoes
juice of 1 orange
500ml (18fl oz) chicken or vegetable stock
salt and pepper
5 bulging handfuls of baby spinach leaves
2 handfuls of coriander leaves
Greek yoghurt, to serve

Cut the preserved lemon into quarters. Scoop out and discard the pulp and finely chop the peel.

Heat the oil in a large saucepan. Stir in the onion and let it cook gently for 6–7 minutes, or until soft and pale gold, then add the garlic, spices and lemon peel and stir for a minute or so more. Tip in the squash and chickpeas and stir everything together so it's thoroughly mixed.

Add the tomatoes, orange juice and stock. Season, and bring to a simmer, then cook, uncovered, over a medium heat for 40–45 minutes, or until the squash is soft, pushing the bits under the surface from time to time. Throw in the spinach and stir through until it is wilted and soft. Season well, tasting as you go – you'll need at least another ¼ teaspoon salt, probably more – then mix in most of the coriander. Pile into bowls, scattering each one with more coriander and adding a blob of Greek yoghurt.

A fish stew with aïoli

This is a rustic bowlful. Don't be put off by the long list of ingredients. Most are just thrown into a big pan together to make a flavoursome stock. I sometimes add a splash of Pernod to the juices while they're cooking, but I'll leave that up to you.

Use whatever white fish you can get your hands on. In my time, I've used pollock, cod, red mullet, sea bream or a mixture.

For 4
4 tbsp olive oil
5 plump garlic cloves, finely chopped
2 medium onions, finely chopped
1 small fennel bulb, finely chopped
4 bushy sprigs of thyme
2 big pinches of saffron threads
a pinch of crushed chilli flakes
5cm (2in) strip of orange peel
4 medium tomatoes, chopped
200ml (7fl oz) dry vermouth or dry white wine
500ml (18fl oz) fish stock
4–6 big handfuls of raw mussels or clams, or a mix of both, scrubbed and
   debearded (see page 108 for details)
600g (1lb 5oz) fillets of white fish, cut into 8
4–8 big raw prawns, optional
sea salt and freshly ground black pepper
a large handful of chopped parsley
a bowl of aïoli (page 254)

Heat the oil in a large saucepan and throw in the garlic, chopped vegetables, thyme, saffron, chilli and orange peel. Cook over a low heat for 6–8 minutes, stirring occasionally, until soft. Add the chopped tomatoes and cook for 5 minutes, then throw in the vermouth, turn up the heat a little, and bubble away for a further 3 minutes. Pour in the fish stock and simmer gently for 10 minutes more.

While the stock is cooking, put the mussels or clams in a small saucepan with 2 tablespoons water, cover with a lid, and cook over a medium heat for 4 minutes until the shells have just opened. Strain the cooking liquid into the big pan and keep the mussels or clams to one side.

When the sauce has done its thing, lay the fish fillets on top, along with the prawns if you're using them, then cover with a lid, and poach over a gentle heat for 6–8 minutes, or until the fish is nearly cooked through. You want it to flake easily when pushed with a fork. Add the mussels or clams, replace the lid, and cook for a minute or so to warm them through. Taste the juices and season.

Pile the stew into bowls, scatter with parsley and eat with a blob of aïoli on the side, stirring it into the sauce as you go. Bread for mopping is essential, as is a bowl for shells in the middle of the table.

Braised lamb shanks with orange

This is a kind of lamb osso bucco, the meat braised in an aromatic sauce of tomato, wine and herbs until it falls lazily from the bone. The orange gremolata, sprinkled over the top at the end, adds an uplifting shot of freshness.

For 4
4 lamb shanks, about 350g–400g (12–14oz) each
salt and freshly ground black pepper
3 tbsp olive oil
1 x 50g (1¾oz) can anchovy fillets in olive oil
2 medium carrots, finely chopped
3 celery sticks, finely chopped
2 medium onions, finely chopped
1 pinch crushed chilli flakes
1 head garlic, halved horizontally
2 bay leaves
10cm (4in) strip of orange peel
3 sprigs of thyme
1 big sprig of rosemary
250ml (9fl oz) dry white wine
1 x 400g (14oz) can plum tomatoes, chopped into small pieces
250ml (9fl oz) chicken stock

For the gremolata
2 garlic cloves, finely chopped
a big handful of flat-leaf parsley, finely chopped
zest of 2 oranges

cont...

Preheat the oven to 160°C/325°F/Gas Mark 3. Season the lamb well.

Heat the oil in an ovenproof casserole dish on the hob. Add the lamb and seal in the hot fat for 10-15 minutes until golden brown on all sides. Remove and put to one side. You may have to do this in batches. Tip out the fat.

Pour in the oil from the can of anchovies (but not the anchovies themselves), along with the carrots, celery and onions. Stir together, then turn down the heat and cook for about 10 minutes, stirring occasionally, until the vegetables have softened. Chop the anchovies and stir into the pan, with the chilli flakes, garlic, bay leaves, orange peel, thyme and rosemary. Pour in the wine, then turn up the heat and bring to a bubble for a couple of minutes. Stir in the tomatoes and stock, then tuck the meat into the liquid. Bring everything to a simmer.

Cover with a bit of crumpled greaseproof paper or baking parchment, then put the lid on the pot and place in the oven for 2–2½ hours, or until the meat is on the verge of falling from the bones, removing the lid for the final 30 minutes. If you want to make it in advance, give it 2 hours one day, then a further 30 minutes the next to reheat it.

Once it's cooked, remove from the oven and leave to cool for 10 minutes. Scoop off some of the fat that has gathered on the surface, then taste the sauce and season again if necessary.

To make the gremolata, combine the garlic, parsley and orange zest and pile it into a small bowl. Serve the stew with mash, scattering some of the gremolata over the top.

Goulash

I associate this with a man called, genuinely, if somewhat implausibly, Herr Pfefferkorn (Mr Peppercorn), who ran a restaurant on a mountainside in the Austrian Alps. He had two fingers missing from his left hand, which, as a child, I found fascinating and dangerous.

My version of goulash is made with pork rather than the more traditional beef. It's a wonderfully peasanty and satisfying stew, with the gentle warmth of paprika, red peppers and caraway. I think it goes just as well on a damp day in Britain as it does with mountain sunshine, dripping icicles and the smell of Ambre Solaire.

Serves 4

100g (3½oz) smoked streaky bacon, cut into small strips
1 tbsp olive oil
3 medium onions, finely sliced
2 red peppers, deseeded and cut into thin strips
3 garlic cloves, crushed
1kg (2lb 4oz) pork shoulder, cut into 2–3cm (¾–1¼in) cubes
2 tbsp tomato purée
1½ tbsp sweet (mild) paprika
a big pinch of cayenne pepper
1 tsp caraway seeds, lightly crushed
150ml (5fl oz) red wine
1 tbsp red wine vinegar
1 bay leaf
salt and pepper
soured cream or Greek yoghurt

Preheat the oven to 140°C/275°F/Gas Mark 1. Put an oven-proof casserole pot on the hob, add the bacon and cook over a medium heat for 2–3 minutes, until it has released its fat. Add the oil and mix in the onions and peppers, then cook over a medium heat, stirring often, for 10 minutes, or until the vegetables are soft and sweet. Stir in the garlic, then add the meat and stir for 5–6 minutes, until it has lost its pink colour. Mix in the tomato purée and stir for a couple of minutes, then sprinkle with the paprika, cayenne and caraway and stir for a couple of minutes more.

Tip in the red wine, vinegar and bay leaf, along with 150ml (5fl oz) water. Season well, bring to a simmer, then cover and put in the oven for 1¾–2 hours. You want the meat to be tender and on the verge of falling apart. Season again, then leave to cool for 15 minutes and spoon off some of the fat. Ladle into bowls and eat with a blob of soured cream or Greek yoghurt on top.

Beef stew with cinnamon and prunes

I first had beef with cinnamon in the Greek stew 'stifado'. The prune idea must, I think, have come from a Moroccan lamb tagine. Together, they will fill your kitchen with beckoning smells. Like all stews, this is better reheated the next day.

For 4
2 tbsp olive oil
1kg (2lb 4oz) shin or chuck of beef, cut into 8 equal cubes
salt and pepper
150g (5½oz) smoked lardons, or smoked streaky bacon, cut into strips
2 medium onions, peeled and finely chopped
4 plump garlic cloves, peeled and roughly chopped
2 tbsp tomato purée
1 big sprig of parsley, plus extra for sprinkling
4 sprigs of thyme
1–2 bay leaves, depending on size
1 tsp ground cumin
2 sticks of cinnamon
2 tbsp red wine vinegar
1 bottle (75cl) red wine
24 ready-to-eat prunes

Preheat the oven to 150°C/300°F/Gas Mark 2. Heat the oil in a casserole over a medium heat. Season the meat and brown in 2–3 batches, for about 6 minutes each, turning so it is browned on all sides. Remove to a bowl or plate and put to one side.

Throw the lardons or bacon into the pot and cook for 1 minute, then add the onions and cook for 5 minutes more, stirring often. Add the garlic and stir in, then add the tomato purée, herbs (tied together as a bouquet garni), ground cumin and cinnamon. Cook for a couple of minutes more, then tip in the vinegar and wine. Add the meat and any juices that have gathered, season well then bring to a simmer and cover the surface of the stew with a circle of greaseproof paper – this will help the meat to stay moist. Put the lid on the pot and place in the oven for 2 hours.

When the two hours are up, stir in the prunes, then leave to cool, preferably overnight.

An hour-and-a-half before you want to eat, heat the oven to 150°C/300°F/Gas Mark 2 again. Warm the stew to a simmer on top of the stove, then put the dish in the oven, without the lid or greaseproof, and cook for 1 hour more. (Have a look after 30 minutes and replace the lid if the liquid has fallen below the level of the meat.) Check the seasoning, then scatter with a bit of finely chopped parsley and serve in bowls on clouds of smooth mash.

There's a simple joy to summer vegetables. From the first eager shoots of asparagus, through lettuces, cucumbers and radishes, to the late glut of tomatoes and courgettes, they offer up a non-stop parade of all that is perky and fresh.

They also make things pretty easy in the kitchen. I get a bit lazy at this time of year. It's not that I care less about what I eat. It's simply that summer food requires more in the way of compilation than actual cooking.

Although some vegetables still need a blast of heat to bring out the best in them, many want nothing more than a splash of good olive oil, a scattering of salt and a squeeze of lemon. And there are plenty of simple combinations that need just as little adornment. I like to think of summer salads as the culinary equivalent of shorts and T-shirts – the kind of throw-together stuff you want for a lazy afternoon in the sun.

Strawberry,
cucumber and
watercress salad

Cucumber
and cantaloupe

Radishes with
butter and salt

Grilled aubergines
with anchovies, mint
and mozzarella

Courgette and
pine nut salad

The joy of
tomato salad

A feast of asparagus

Three potato salads

Ruby chard with
lemon and feta

Summer
salads

Strawberry, cucumber and watercress salad

I first read about the combination of strawberries and cucumber in Jane Grigson's 'Vegetable Book'. It's a wonderful summer partnership, called Salad Elona. The watercress adds another, peppery dimension. This would be good with some cold chicken or soft, fresh cream cheese.

For 4
1 large cucumber, cut lengthways into strips with a peeler, ideally avoiding the seeds
500g (1lb 2oz) strawberries, hulled and thinly sliced
4 big handfuls of watercress leaves
1 tbsp white wine vinegar
1 tsp caster sugar
1 handful of torn mint leaves
extra-virgin olive oil
sea salt and pepper

Arrange the cucumber, strawberries and watercress on a large serving plate. Mix together the vinegar and sugar and sprinkle over the salad, then scatter the mint leaves over the top. Add a splash of oil and season well, being particularly generous with the black pepper.

Cucumber and cantaloupe

A cooling combination of summer flavours, and the closest thing to liquid refreshment you can get in a salad. The cantaloupe brings out the cucumber's melon-like qualities.

For 4
1 ripe canteloupe melon, halved and deseeded
1 large cucumber, peeled
2 tsp white wine vinegar
sea salt and black pepper
2 small handfuls of mint leaves
extra-virgin olive oil

Divide each melon half into 4. Cut off the peel, then slice each piece into rough half-moons. Halve the cucumber lengthways, then cut across into slices roughly 3mm (⅛in) thick. Arrange the melon and cucumber in a large bowl or on a wide plate and sprinkle over 2 tsp of white wine vinegar.

Season with about ½ teaspoon of sea-salt flakes and a few coarse grinds of black pepper, then scatter the mint leaves over the top, tearing any large ones. Sprinkle with 2–3 tablespoons extra-virgin olive oil and serve.

Radishes with butter and salt

This is something for late spring and summer, when bunches of young, torpedo-shaped radishes appear in the shops. The French way of eating them, with hard butter and a sprinkling of salt, adds up to deliciously more than the sum of its parts. The leaves can be a bit rough, but if they are fresh and unblemished, I often eat them as well, dipping them into a pot of dressing. They have a flavour that can only be described as leafy.

For 4
4 bunches radishes, with their leaves attached
cold, lightly salted butter
sea salt flakes and fresh black pepper
crusty French bread
a bowl of mustard dressing (page 256), optional

Wash the radishes and their leaves well, getting rid of any dirt. Drain thoroughly and arrange on a large plate, with their leaves trailing behind them. Encourage people to take a slab of butter and a pile of salt and then either butter a hunk of baguette (fresh or toasted) and slice the radishes on top with a pinch of salt and pepper; or nibble, smear and dunk each individual radish – as the mood takes them. As for the leaves, it's a personal thing, but I tend to dunk them in dressing, then drape them on a bit of bread.

Grilled aubergines with anchovies, mint and mozzarella

I love the contrasts here: creamy charred aubergine and salty anchovy, cool mozzarella and vivid mint. This would be great with some grilled lamb chops or on its own as a lightish lunch.

For 4
4 big handfuls of mint leaves
2 garlic cloves, crushed
2 tsp red wine vinegar
100ml (3½fl oz) extra-virgin olive oil, plus extra for brushing
salt and pepper
500g (1lb 2oz) medium-sized aubergines
2 x 125g (4½oz) balls of buffalo mozzarella
1 x 50g (1¾oz) can anchovies in oil, drained

In a food processor, blitz the mint with the garlic and vinegar, then add the olive oil and whizz again to give a green-flecked dressing. Season well.

Cut the aubergine lengthways into slices about 5mm (¼in) thick. Unless the aubergines are very skinny, cut each slice in half lengthways. Put a ridged stove-top grill pan or similar heavy frying pan on the hob and heat for 4–5 minutes. Brush the aubergine slices lightly with oil on both sides and grill in batches in the preheated pan for 3 minutes each side, or until the flesh is softly yielding and patterned with black lines. Press them down as they cook so the whole surface gets a fair go at the heat. As each batch is done, tip it into a bowl and season – the aubergine will soften a bit more as it cools.

Arrange the aubergine slices on a wide plate and tear the mozzarella over the top. Season, then add the strips of anchovy and a few splashes of mint oil.

Courgette and pine nut salad

The simplest of thrown-together salads: green and zesty with a bit of crunch. I think it's particularly good with grilled or roast chicken.

For 4
2 handfuls of pine nuts
750g (1lb 10oz) small courgettes, green, yellow, or a mixture
salt and pepper
1 garlic clove, crushed
finely grated zest of 1 lemon and some of the juice
3 tbsp extra-virgin olive oil
2 handfuls of basil leaves, torn
a few shavings of Parmesan

Throw the pine nuts into a dry frying pan and stir over the heat for a few minutes until tinged with gold.

Using a potato peeler, shave the courgettes lengthways into strips about 2–3cm (¾–1¼in) wide, leaving behind the seedy core – turn the courgettes each time you hit the core and continue shaving the next side. Toss the ribbons with 1 teaspoon salt and leave to drain in a colander for 30 minutes. This helps to get rid of any bitterness. Not all courgettes need it, but it won't hurt. When they've had their time, rinse well and either pat dry or gently squeeze to get rid of the liquid.

Mix the strips of courgette with the garlic, lemon zest and 2 tablespoons of the olive oil, adding as much of the lemon juice as you think it needs. Stir in half the basil and half the toasted pine nuts and season well with pepper, plus some salt if necessary, then leave to stand for a few minutes for the flavours to mingle. Scatter the remaining basil leaves and pine nuts over the top, along with a few shavings of Parmesan. Splash with the remaining oil, grind over a little more pepper and serve.

The joy of tomato salad

One summer, I lived near a convenience store that sold mostly fags and mags, but in the window was a small display of fruit and vegetables. The greenhouse heat didn't do much for the apples, which were sadly woolly and wizened, but it transformed the boxes of otherwise joyless tomatoes, turning them sweet and scarlet. I spent that summer eating endless variations on a tomato salad theme. Few things are as perfect, when the tomatoes are good.

I think a properly ripe tomato needs little more than good olive oil and salt. If your tomatoes are a bit on the bland and un-summery side, you might want a tiny splash of vinegar (red wine vinegar would be my preference, though use balsamic if you're of an Italian bent) and maybe a tiny pinch of sugar. Often, though, the tomatoes' own sweet-acid juices are enough.

Anyway, this is how I go about making my tomato salad. It's not so much a recipe as a blueprint.

For as few or as many as you want
ripe, sweet, flavourful tomatoes (big, small, red, yellow, brown or a mix),
  sliced or halved if they're very small
sea salt and pepper
a pinch of sugar, optional
extra-virgin olive oil and red wine vinegar or balsamic vinegar,
  or mustard dressing (page 256)
mint leaves (whole or torn) or basil leaves (whole, torn or shredded) or
  tarragon leaves (left whole and strewn)
chopped red onion or spring onion or shallot or chives
  (and chive flowers) or some crushed garlic
anchovies, optional
rough cubes of bread, optional

Arrange the tomatoes on a wide plate and strew with sea salt flakes and a bit of ground pepper. Please don't, whatever you do, forget the salt. Salt brings tomatoes to life. Taste one beforehand and decide if sugar might be a welcome addition. If so, add the merest pinch.

Splash the tomatoes generously with oil, so it mingles with the tomato juices. You may be finished. But you may also want to add a few drops of red wine vinegar or balsamic. Or you may want to splash your tomatoes with mustard dressing instead.

I often scatter some herbs over the top: mint or basil usually, but sometimes a few tarragon leaves – and add a contrasting sprinkle of something oniony. Sometimes, I'll add a few torn anchovies (with basil or mint) and occasionally I'll turn it into a panzanella-ish salad, tossing it all together with some cubes of rustic bread, with an extra splash of red wine vinegar and oil, and tucking in quickly, while the bread is no longer hard but hasn't yet turned to pulp.

A feast of asparagus

During the brief and blissful home-grown asparagus season – between late April and the end of June – I eat the stuff on average at least twice a week. The shoots that push their way up through Britain's springtime soil have a vigorous freshness that you simply don't get with imported. I always think it's like eating a mouthful of chlorophyll.

For boiled or steamed asparagus, a puddle of silken sauce – made with butter, eggs or both – is the best accompaniment, and I've given you some variations on pages 198–9. Occasionally, though, I just dunk the tips into a bowl of vinaigrette.

Between four people, 500g (1lb 2oz) of asparagus is a treat; 1kg (2lb 4oz) is a feast. Make your sauce before you cook the spears.

For 4
500g–1kg (1lb 2oz–2lb 4oz) slender green asparagus
Hollandaise, butter and balsamic, melted butter or orange sauce, to serve

Snap the asparagus stems in half – they naturally break at the point where they are uniformly tender, so if you use only the spear end, you avoid any stringiness. Don't throw away the bottom: you can use them to make stock for an asparagus soup or risotto. Very slender stems may just need trimming at the base, rather than snapping.

Bring a big saucepan of water to the boil over a high heat, then throw in the asparagus spears. Return to a simmer and cook for 3–6 minutes, depending on their size. The slenderest stems – those about 5mm (¼in) thick – will need only the shortest cooking time, while those as fat as a finger will need 5–6 minutes. Add them in stages if necessary. Once they're cooked, drain well and pile onto plates (or into a communal bowl) and serve with one of the following sauces.

cont…

Each sauce serves 4

Hollandaise sauce

I make this the cheat's way, I'm afraid, in a blender. The only possible downside is that the egg yolks aren't entirely cooked in the process, so, if you're young or frail or pregnant, the same rules apply as with homemade mayonnaise.

250g (9oz) butter
4 medium egg yolks
juice of 1 lemon, maybe a bit more
cayenne pepper
salt and black pepper

Fill the blender with just boiled water and leave it to warm it a little. In a small saucepan, melt the butter until it's hot and bubbling – a saucepan with a spout is best, as you'll need to pour the butter later.

Empty the hot water from the blender and quickly shake dry. Put the yolks in the blender with the juice of ½ lemon and blitz for 30 seconds. Quickly reheat the butter, then, with the blender running, very slowly and gradually pour onto the egg yolks in a thin stream. You want the whole pouring process to last about 20 seconds.

The sauce should become thick and smooth. Add a good pinch of cayenne and some salt – how much will depend on the saltiness or otherwise of your butter. Whizz that in, then taste the sauce and add some more of the lemon juice – you may not need all of it or you may need a bit extra; see what you think. Grind in a bit of black pepper and whizz again. Finally, add 1 tablespoon boiling water and blend in. This will help keep the sauce stable. Taste and season again with salt and lemon as you see fit.

You can keep the sauce warm for about 20 minutes in a metal bowl suspended over a pan of hot (but turned off) water. Far easier, though, is to pour the sauce into a vacuum flask, where it will keep warm for a good couple of hours until you need it.

Butter and balsamic

100g (3½oz) butter
salt and black pepper
good balsamic vinegar

Melt the butter, seasoning as necessary. Leave to stand for a minute, then pour over the tips of the asparagus, leaving the white milk solids in the pan. Add a few dots of balsamic – literally about ½ teaspoon per plate – which will mingle deliciously with the butter.

Melted butter

100g (3½oz) butter
salt and black pepper

As above – just don't add the balsamic vinegar.

Orange butter sauce

juice of 1 orange and the zest of one half
4 tbsp dry white wine
1 small shallot, finely chopped
1 tbsp double cream
100g (3½oz) cold butter, cut into small pieces
salt and black pepper

Put the orange juice, wine and chopped shallot in a small saucepan. Bring to a simmer and bubble over a strong heat until there's only about 1 tablespoon left (this will take 3–5 minutes). Turn the heat down low, then whisk in the cream.

Now, off the heat, add the butter, a piece at a time, swirling the pan to melt each one before throwing in the next. When the sauce is smooth and glossy, stir in the orange zest and season well.

Three potato salads

Potato salad goes with everything from cold chicken to hot hamburgers. I particularly like it with a schnitzel. I've given you three variations, all quite different, so you can match them to your mood and whatever else you're eating.

Each makes enough for 4
750g (1lb 10oz) waxy new potatoes, evenly sized

Boil the potatoes in salted water for 20 minutes, or until soft right the way through (cut one in half to check). When they're done, drain well and use in one of the following.

A simple, vaguely Germanic version
1 tbsp Dijon mustard
2 tbsp red wine vinegar
½ tsp caster sugar
salt and pepper
2 tbsp extra-virgin olive oil
5 tbsp groundnut or sunflower oil
3 handfuls of chives, chopped
2 big handfuls of fresh dill, chopped
1 big dill pickled cucumber, chopped

Leave the potatoes to cool a little. Peel off the skins (they should come away easily if you spear them with a fork and scrape at them gently with the tip of a knife). Cut into 1cm (½in) slices and put in a salad bowl.

Mix together the mustard, red wine vinegar and sugar with some salt and pepper. Gradually beat in the oils. Pour the dressing over the potatoes while they are still warm, then stir in the chives, dill and pickled cucumber and leave for 1–2 hours for the flavours to become acquainted. Scatter more dill or chives over the top if you want. Eat cold or at room temperature.

A green herb version with rocket

salsa verde (page 255)
3 handfuls of rocket
salt and pepper
extra-virgin olive oil
a handful of mint leaves

While the potatoes are cooking, make the salsa verde. Cut the drained
potatoes into halves, quarters or eighths, depending on their size. Put in a
salad bowl and stir in the salsa verde while they are still warm. Leave to cool
to room temperature – or chill in the fridge – before stirring in the rocket
(or eat it slightly warm with the rocket wilted into the potatoes at the same
time as you add the sauce). Check the seasoning and add a good glug more
olive oil. Toss together and scatter the mint leaves over the top.

A creamy, beany version

1 tbsp wholegrain mustard
2 tbsp red wine vinegar
2 tbsp olive oil, plus extra to serve
½ red onion, finely chopped
salt and pepper
250g (9oz) green beans, topped and tailed
150ml (5fl oz) crème fraîche
1 tbsp lemon juice
1 celery stick, finely chopped
2 tbsp chopped tarragon

Cut the drained potatoes into halves, quarters or eighths, depending on their
size. Put them in a salad bowl. Whisk together the mustard, vinegar, oil and
red onion. Season well, then pour over the potatoes while they are still warm.

Meanwhile, cut the beans in half across the middle and throw them into a
pan of boiling salted water. Cook for 4–5 minutes, or until just tender, then
drain in a colander and run under the cold top until cool.

Mix the crème fraîche with the lemon juice, then stir loosely into the
potatoes, along with the celery, beans and tarragon. Add a splash more
olive oil on top if you fancy it.

Ruby chard with lemon and feta

You get all sorts of flavours going on here: salt, sharp, sweet, earthy.
I have rather a thing about chard. I love the iron-rich taste and dual textures
of leaf and rib. You don't, of course, need to use ruby or rainbow chard – it
just adds a swirl of colour.

Serves 2

300g (10½oz) ruby or rainbow chard, washed and trimmed
extra-virgin olive oil
½ red onion, finely sliced
2 plump garlic cloves, finely sliced
sea salt and pepper
juice of 1 lemon and zest of ½
2–3 tbsp raisins
75g (2¾oz) feta

Separate the chard stalks and leaves. Chop the stalks about 1cm (½in) thick
and tear up the leaves.

In a saucepan, heat a couple of tablespoons of oil. Throw in the onion and
garlic and sweat over a gentle heat for 5 minutes, or until soft and sweet
but not brown. Add the chard stalks, some salt and pepper and the lemon
juice. Toss everything together, then cover the pan with a lid and cook for
4 minutes. Now, stir in the raisins and chard leaves, turn up the heat, and
stir for another 5–6 minutes, or until the ribs are tender and the leaves
wilted and soft.

Remove from the heat, toss in the lemon zest and leave to cool until
lukewarm. Dress with a good glug of extra-virgin olive oil, check the
seasoning and add more lemon juice if you think it needs it. Crumble
some feta over the top and add a drizzle more oil before serving.

Outside my window, the rain has drawn a curtain across the sky. It's the middle of August. On days like this, you can understand why gazpacho was invented in Spain and not Britain. But when the sun comes out to play, few things are as refreshing as a chilled soup. On a sultry afternoon, it can be every bit as cooling as an ice cream or a slice of melon.

Even so, we have a slight mistrust of cold soups in this country. It's like the old joke about Vichyssoise – that it was very nice but could have done with being a bit warmer. There's a common misapprehension that chilled soup is simply hot soup served cold. But it's actually a totally different creature. Vichyssoise would be nastily gloopy if it were as thick as its cold-weather counterpart. The consistency of summer soups needs to be altogether thinner and more delicate, which is why so many of them start off with 'liquid' ingredients such as cucumber, lettuce or tomatoes.

Puréed soups do, though, thicken up as they cool, so be prepared to thin them down a little after they've been in the fridge. They also need a robust hand with the seasoning, particularly the salt. Like us, flavours are numbed by cold.

If the weather happens to bring more showers than sunshine, many of these soups can, paradoxically, be served warm. I've also included one soup – more of a broth really – that's deliberately hot, with bright, summer flavours to cheer you on cloudy days

Cucumber
gazpacho

Chilled pea,
lettuce and
tarragon soup

Celery
vichyssoise

Chilled tomato
and cumin soup

Summer
vegetable
broth with
pesto

Summer
soup

Cucumber gazpacho

Cucumbers have an elusive green flavour and perfume that are quite unlike anything else. Combined with its curious cooling properties, it's what makes this soup so refreshing.

For 4

4 big cucumbers (each about as long as your forearm)
salt and pepper
2 garlic cloves, crushed
1 celery stick, finely chopped
1 tsp ground cumin
a small pinch of crushed chilli flakes
2 tbsp white wine vinegar
125ml (4fl oz) Greek yoghurt
a squeeze of lemon juice
100ml (3½fl oz) extra-virgin olive oil, plus a bit more for sprinkling
a few small mint leaves

Peel the cucumbers, cut them in half lengthways, then scoop out the seeds with a spoon. Keep back one-quarter of a cucumber and roughly chop the rest. Place in a colander and sprinkle with 2 teaspoons salt. Toss together, then leave to stand for 20 minutes to rid the cucumbers of some of their bitterness. Tip into a sieve and rinse under the tap.

Mix the rinsed cucumbers with everything except the mint leaves, and whizz in batches for a few seconds until everything is blended. Check the seasoning – remembering that things taste less salty when they're chilled – and add a squeeze more lemon, if you feel it needs it, then put in the fridge for 2–3 hours to chill.

Ladle the soup into bowls. Cut the remaining cucumber into small cubes and scatter a few into the centre of each bowl, then add a grind of black pepper and a few extra drops of oil. Scatter a few mint leaves over the top.

Chilled pea, lettuce and tarragon soup

A silken green soup with a natural sweetness. I could eat this every day throughout the summer. Using frozen peas is fine, by the way. In fact, they are likely to be better than fresh unless you've plucked your peas from the plant yourself.

For 4
2 tbsp butter
½ medium onion, peeled and finely chopped
1 litre (1¾ pints) vegetable stock
500g (1lb 2oz) shelled or frozen peas
leaves from 4 bushy sprigs of tarragon, plus a few extra leaves for decoration
250g (9oz) romaine lettuce
pinch of sugar
salt and pepper
crème fraîche

Melt the butter in a large saucepan and add the onion. Cook over a gentle heat for 5 minutes or so, stirring occasionally, until the onion has softened slightly. Add the stock and bring to a simmer, then throw in the peas, tarragon and lettuce, plus a good pinch of sugar. Stir in well and cook for about 10 minutes until tender. Remove the pan from the heat.

Drain off the liquid into a jug and keep to one side. Tip half the vegetables into a blender, add a ladleful of the stock and blitz to a smooth purée. Add half the remaining stock and blitz again. Tip into a large bowl and keep to one side. Whizz the remaining vegetables and stock in the same way and stir together with the first batch. Season well and put in the fridge to chill.

Once it's cold, check the seasoning again – it may need a bit more salt. Ladle into bowls and and eat with a blob of crème fraîche on top and some extra tarragon leaves scattered over for decoration.

Celery vichyssoise

The celery gives this chilled soup a faintly spicy edge. If you want to amplify its charms, you could pile a spoonful of white crab meat or some cooked coldwater prawns in the middle of each bowl. You can also eat it hot – just leave out the milk and the radish.

For 4
25g (1oz) butter
2 medium leeks, white part only, finely chopped
½ medium onion, peeled and finely chopped
5 celery sticks, finely chopped, plus some of the young leaves
1 medium potato, peeled and finely chopped
salt and pepper
500ml (18fl oz) chicken stock
150ml (5fl oz) single cream
100–150ml (3½–5fl oz) cold milk
2 radishes
a few chopped chives

Melt the butter in a large saucepan and add the chopped leeks, onion, celery and potato. Add a good pinch of salt and stir everything together until it's well coated in the butter. Cover with a lid and cook over a gentle heat for 15 minutes, or until the vegetables are soft, giving things an occasional stir to stop it from sticking.

Add the stock, bring to a boil, then reduce the heat and simmer, without a lid, for about 20 minutes. Remove from the heat and stir in the cream. Blitz with a hand-held electric blender or a liquidiser until totally smooth. (Do this in batches, or you risk splattering the kitchen.) Then pour through a sieve over a large bowl. Push everything through using the domed side of a ladle, until all that's left in the sieve are a few tablespoonfuls of the most fibrous bits of vegetable. This takes only a minute or two.

Season well and chill in the fridge until you want to eat. Thin it with a bit of milk before serving. Exactly how much depends on the thickening power of your potato, but you want the end result to be on the thin side – a bit like pourable double cream. Cold thick soup isn't a good thing.

Thinly slice the radishes, then cut the slices into thin strips. Ladle the soup into bowls and scatter some of the radish sticks into the centre of each one, along with a few young celery leaves, a restrained sprinkling of chopped chives and a grind or two of black pepper.

Chilled tomato and cumin soup

I think of cumin as a sort of magic bullet where soup is concerned. There are few vegetables that aren't given a lift by its zestful earthiness. This is a soup for late summer, when tomatoes are ripe and sweet and actually taste of something. I prefer it chilled – it has the slight kick of a good Bloody Mary – but if the temperature suddenly makes a bid for the North Pole, you can always warm it gently on the stove. I've also given a version using canned tomatoes, for times when fresh ones taste of nothing but cold water and cotton wool.

For 4
1kg (2lb 4oz) flavourful baby plum or cherry tomatoes, halved
6 tbsp olive oil
sea salt flakes and pepper
1 medium red onion, finely chopped
1 celery stick, finely chopped
a good pinch of crushed chilli flakes
2 tsp ground cumin, plus extra for sprinkling
4 garlic cloves, crushed
750ml (1¼ pints) vegetable stock
½ tsp caster sugar
Greek yoghurt

Preheat the oven to 180°C/350°F/Gas Mark 4. Scatter the halved tomatoes in a large roasting tray and sprinkle with half the oil and a couple of pinches of sea salt. Put in the oven for 45 minutes.

Meanwhile, heat the remaining oil in a big saucepan and add the onion, celery and chilli. Turn down the heat and let everything cook gently for 15 minutes, stirring occasionally, until the vegetables are soft and sweet. Add the cumin and garlic and stir through for a couple of minutes, then tip in the roasted tomatoes, along with the juices and oil from the roasting tray. Pour in the stock and bring back to a bubble.

Blitz until smooth – you'll need to do this in two batches if you're using a liquidiser – then rub the whole thing quickly through a sieve, so the seeds and tough skins are left behind. This sounds like a faff, but it takes only a minute or two. Scrape any purée off the bottom of the sieve.

Leave to cool, then put in the fridge to chill for a couple of hours. Check the seasoning and ladle into bowls. Serve each one with a blob of yoghurt in the middle and an extra sprinkling of cumin.

cont…

When fresh tomatoes aren't so hot …

Cook the onion, celery and chilli in 4 tablespoons of olive oil, as before, then throw in the cumin and garlic and stir through for a couple of minutes. Add 1 teaspoon sugar, plus two 400g (14oz) cans of chopped plum tomatoes and simmer for 20 minutes, stirring occasionally to break everything up. Tip in the stock and cook for 30 minutes more. Whizz until smooth with a blender or eat just as it is – hot or cold.

Summer vegetable broth with pesto

An uplifting soup, inspired by the Provencal 'soupe au pistou', but made without the traditional pulses, so the whole thing is fresher and lighter. The vegetables require a few minutes concerted chopping. I always approach it as a form of therapy.

For 4–6
3 ripe medium tomatoes
4 big handfuls of basil leaves
50g (1¾oz) Parmesan, grated
4 garlic cloves, crushed
extra-virgin olive oil
1 medium onion, finely chopped
1 celery stick, finely chopped
1 medium carrot, finely chopped
1 medium leek, finely chopped
salt and pepper
250g (9oz) courgette, cut into 5mm (¼in) cubes
3 small new potatoes, cut into 5mm (¼in) cubes
1 litre (1¾ pints) chicken or vegetable stock
2 big handfuls of green beans, topped, tailed and finely chopped

Cut the tomatoes into quarters and remove the seeds, then chop the flesh into small cubes. Put a quarter of the tomato into a food processor with the basil, Parmesan and garlic. Keep the remaining tomato to one side. Add 3 tablespoons olive oil to the basil mixture and whizz to make a chunky pesto. Keep to one side.

Heat 1 tablespoon oil in a large saucepan and throw in the onion, celery, carrot and leek. Add a pinch of salt, stir everything together, and cook over a gentle heat for 5–6 minutes, stirring occasionally, until the vegetables are starting to soften. Throw in the courgettes and potatoes, and cook for a couple of minutes more.

Pour in the stock, plus 250ml (9fl oz) water, bring everything to a simmer and leave things to bubble away for 10 minutes, or until the bits of potato are soft.

Add the beans and reserved tomatoes and simmer for another 5 minutes, then stir in half the pesto. Season well and leave to stand for 10 minutes, so the flavours can get acquainted. Have a taste and season again if necessary. Ladle into bowls, adding a small blob of the remaining pesto to each one, plus an extra splash of olive oil, if you like.

When I was little, I had a favourite picture book: 'Patrick', by Quentin Blake. It told the story of a man who had a magic violin and, when he played, strange and beautiful things happened. Fish flew, cows danced in the fields and a tramp blew fireworks from his pipe. The bit I liked most – the bit I've always vividly remembered – was the moment when the branches of an old apple tree were suddenly and gloriously filled with food. There were cakes, jellies, ice cream and, best of all, slices of hot buttered toast, which dripped into the open mouth of a small boy standing underneath. I wanted to be that boy. Toast was part of my hungriest imaginings.

It was also a staple of our childhood teatimes, a reward and comfort after the blustering walk from the school bus. There was toast and honey, toast and jam, toast and tomatoes, toast and beans. And, sometimes, my dad's greatest – and perhaps only – culinary invention, the instant pizza: toast topped with melted cheese and the tomato sauce from last night's spaghetti. Everything always tasted better on toast.

I think it probably still does.

Peas, broad beans
and ricotta on toast

Lemon curd

Cream cheese,
anchoïade and
basil on toast

Somerset rarebit

Mackerel, mustard
and cucumber
on toast

Devilled kidneys
and watercress

Roast tomatoes
and mozzarella

Things
on toast

Peas, broad beans and ricotta on toast

Vibrant and green, with a gentle sweetness, this is like eating a mouthful of early summer.

For 2
2 handfuls of podded broad beans
2 handfuls of fresh or frozen peas
extra-virgin olive oil
salt and pepper
2 big pieces of rustic toast
1 garlic clove, halved
6 tbsp ricotta
20 small mint leaves

Bring a small saucepan of water to the boil. Throw in the beans, bring back to the boil and cook for 3 minutes, then add the peas and cook for 3 minutes more. Drain into a sieve and run under the cold tap for a minute or so until cold. Pick out the broad beans and gently pinch them between your fingers at one end, so the vivid green coins slide from the sage-coloured skins. It takes only a few minutes and makes the experience of eating broad beans much more attractive. Tip into a small bowl with the peas, a splash of olive oil and some salt and pepper and toss together until everything is coated.

Rub the toast with the cut side of the garlic to give it some flavour. Sprinkle the surface with olive oil, then pile the ricotta on top. Add a mound of peas and beans, then tear some of the mint leaves over the top. Add a splash more oil and a generous grinding of pepper.

Lemon curd

I thought about giving you a jam recipe here, but homemade lemon curd is so easy to make – and so much better than the stuff in the shops – that it seemed the obvious choice. And, to be honest, I'm far from being the world's best jam maker.

This is a particularly zesty curd and very good on toast. I recommend eating it scone-style, with a blob of something creamy on top. But it's good for, well, anything really: try stirring it through yoghurt or use it to fill a cake.

Makes 2 x 450g (1lb) jars

cont…

juice and very finely grated zest of 6 unwaxed lemons
300g (10½oz) caster sugar
150g (5½oz) cold unsalted butter, cut into cubes
3 medium eggs and 3 medium egg yolks
salt
toast
whipped or clotted cream, or mascarpone, optional

Put the lemon juice, zest, sugar and butter in a heatproof bowl that fits the top of a saucepan. Fill the pan with 2–3cm (¾ –1 ¼in) of water and place the bowl on top, making sure the bottom doesn't touch the water. Turn on the heat and stir until everything has melted together, then, using a whisk, beat in the eggs and egg yolks with a pinch of salt. Cook over just simmering water for 10 minutes or so, whisking often, until the mixture is thick and smooth. Remove from the heat and leave to cool, giving it an occasional whisk to stop a skin from forming.

Spoon into sterilised jars and keep in the fridge until it's needed; it will last for up to a fortnight. Slather the curd onto toast, thinly or thickly as your sensibilities dictate, adding thick cream if you're feeling particularly extravagant.

Cream cheese, anchoïade and basil on toast

When cream cheese meets anchovy, olives and garlic, something incredible happens. Putting them on toast only adds to the experience. You might like to use one of those mild, rindless young goat's cheeses that taste fresh and clean and slightly lemony, though there would be no shame in using Philadelphia.

I've given specific quantities for the anchoïade, but I'll leave the rest up to your appetite.

Makes more than enough anchoïade for 4

For the anchoïade:
6 canned anchovy fillets in olive oil
2 garlic cloves
a handful of pitted black olives
a handful of flat-leaf parsley, chopped
a squeeze of lemon juice
5 tbsp extra-virgin olive oil

cream cheese (or mild, rindless goat's cheese)
toast
a few basil leaves

In a small food processor, whizz together all the ingredients for the anchoïade to give a coarse paste – you may need to scrape down the sides a little and blitz it again. Spread the cheese roughly onto the toast and dribble the anchovy paste over the top. Scatter with some torn basil leaves. I sometimes add an extra splash of olive oil. Up to you.

Somerset rarebit

Like other rarebits – or rabbits – this is really just posh cheese on toast. I find it comes into its own late at night. There are more rarebits out there than you might think. The Welsh one has found fame, but I've also seen recipes for a Scotch version made with blue cheese and stout; an English rarebit, where the toast is soaked in red wine; and an Irish one with chopped gherkins and herbs. This is my Somerset tribute version, using cider, Cheddar and apples. The better your booze, cheese and fruit, the better it will be.

For 4
2 tbsp butter
1 onion, peeled and coarsely grated
salt and pepper
2 tbsp plain flour
200ml (7fl oz) good dry cider
2 tsp wholegrain mustard
250g (9oz) strong West country farmhouse Cheddar, grated
4 well-browned pieces of toast
2 eating apples, cored and sliced

Melt the butter in a medium non-stick saucepan, then add the grated onion and a good pinch of salt. Cook over a gentle heat, stirring often, for about 5 minutes until the onion has softened, but not browned. Sprinkle the flour over the top and stir in for a minute or two more until it starts to turn a pale gold, then gradually beat in the cider until the sauce is smooth – a whisk is good here, to avoid lumps. When you've added all the cider, bring to a boil, then turn down the heat a little and bubble for another 5 minutes. Give it an occasional stir to stop it sticking.

Beat in the mustard, then stir in the cheese until everything is thoroughly melted. Remove from the heat, taste (carefully – it's hot) and season. You can leave it to cool at this stage and keep it in the fridge for a couple of days until you need it.

When you want to eat, heat the grill, spread half the mixture thickly onto your pieces of toast and cover with a layer of overlapping apple slices. Spoon the rest of the rarebit mixture over the top and grill for a 1–2 minutes, or until the top is bubbling and speckled with brown.

Mackerel, mustard and cucumber on toast

Mackerel can take a bit of heat and mustard is a happy playmate.
The cucumber and crème fraîche add a balancing coolness.

For 2
2 mackerel fillets, pin bones removed
extra-virgin olive oil
sea salt and pepper
2 big slices of bread, preferably sourdough
a good 1 tsp Dijon mustard
100g (3½oz) crème fraîche
½ cucumber, sliced wafer thin
2 peppery red radishes, finely sliced
2–3 tbsp finely chopped red onion
4 tbsp chopped dill
2 lemon quarters, for squeezing

Run your finger down the middle of the fillets and pull out any remaining
bones. Use your fingernails if you have them. I'm afraid I'm a bit of a
nibbler, so I generally resort to tweezers. Slash the skin side of the fillet
5–6 times, rub it with oil and season well on both sides.

Put a non-stick frying pan on the hob to heat. Add the fillets, skin side
down, and cook over a medium heat for 3 minutes, then turn them over and
cook for another 1–2 minutes, or until cooked through. Don't stress over it:
mackerel can take harder cooking than most other fish.

Meanwhile, make the toast. Spread each piece with the mustard, then
blob on two thirds of the crème fraîche. Arrange the cucumber and radish
haphazardly on top, season well, and scatter with half the red onion and dill.
Splash with a bit of olive oil, then add the cooked mackerel, skin side up.
Add the remaining crème fraîche, onion and dill, season again, then splash
with a little more oil. Squeeze over some lemon before you eat.

Devilled kidneys and watercress

Devilled kidneys are one of those old-fashioned British things that seem to have made a comeback in recent years. I like the idea of serving them for breakfast or that lost Victorian meal, high tea.

Serves 2
6 lamb's kidneys
salt and pepper
olive oil
2 shallots, peeled and finely chopped
a knob of butter
2 good pinches of cayenne pepper
2 tsp Dijon mustard
1 tbsp red wine vinegar
5 tbsp double cream
3 handfuls of watercress
hot, buttered toast
lemon quarters, to serve

If the kidneys are still covered in a veil-like membrane, puncture it with the point of a knife and peel it away. Slice the kidneys in half lengthways and, using a sharp knife or a pair of scissors, carefully cut away the white gristle from the middle. Try to get rid of it all, or the kidneys will be tough.

Cut each half-kidney into two or three pieces and season well with salt and pepper.

Heat a splash of oil in a frying pan, add the shallots and soften over a medium heat for a couple of minutes. Throw in a good knob of butter, turn up the heat a bit, then add the kidneys and cook for 1½ minutes each side. Stir in the cayenne, mustard and vinegar (watch your eyes, vinegar steam can be vicious). Bubble for a few seconds, then stir in the cream. Cook for another 1–2 minutes, or until the sauce has thickened and the kidneys are cooked through, then remove from the heat and stir in half the watercress. Taste and season again if necessary, then pile on to the hot, buttered toast. Squeeze a bit of lemon juice over the top and scatter the remaining watercress on and around the kidneys. Dive in.

Roast tomatoes and mozzarella

This is a sort of warm Salad Caprese on toast. The fresh cheese mingles with the sweet herby juices from the tomatoes in the most scrumptious way.

For 4
400g (14oz) cherry or baby plum tomatoes
1 garlic clove, crushed
4 bushy sprigs of thyme
salt and pepper
extra-virgin olive oil
4 pieces of toast
2 x 125g (4½oz) balls of buffalo mozzarella
a handful of basil leaves

Preheat the oven to 180°C/350°F/Gas Mark 4.

Halve the tomatoes and arrange them, cut side up, in a roasting tin. Dab each half with some of the crushed garlic, then scatter with the leaves from 3 of the sprigs of thyme. Season well and splash with a few good glugs of the olive oil. Put the tin in the oven and cook for 20–25 minutes, or until the tomatoes are collapsingly juicy and hot.

Pile onto the pieces of toast with some torn-off chunks of mozzarella. Scatter with the remaining thyme leaves, then add a splash more olive oil and some salt and pepper. Tear the basil leaves over the top.

Winter isn't, perhaps, the most obvious time to think about salad. So many of the things we take for granted in summer either clock off for the colder months or simply aren't worth eating.

There are, though, moments in the depths of winter when salad is what I want, which generally means looking beyond the usual suspects. Some of the alternatives are obvious: chicory and cabbage, for instance, are winter's answer to lettuce, crisp and juicy and refreshingly bitter. And fruit – whether the crunch of apples and pears or the bright acidity of citrus – will, with the right partners, happily play a more savoury role.

Roots and tubers might seem better suited to mashes and soups, but everything from Jerusalem artichokes to sweet potatoes and parsnips can be drafted in for salad service. Beetroot, in particular, works well with other seasonal flavours: grated raw into carrot and orange, or roasted and stirred through a bowl of lentils. And don't forget celeriac. It may not be much to look at, but it has a rooty astringency that's as good in a winter slaw as it is in a classic rémoulade – cut into matchsticks and tossed with a mustard mayonnaise.

Of course, there might be some among you who can't quite get your head around the idea of fruit and roots in a salad. Don't worry, I've thrown in one that's pretty much all meat.

Cold rare roast
beef with dill
and mustard

Leeks vinaigrette
with tarragon and
hazelnuts

Winter slaw

Duck breast,
pear and
blue cheese

Celeriac and
beetroot salad

Prawn, chicory
and grapefruit salad

Purple sprouting
Caesar salad

Roast sweet
potato and goat's
cheese salad

Winter
salads

Cold rare roast beef with dill and mustard

Dill and beef are a good partnership and it's a pity that most people put them together only when they slice a pickle into a hamburger. Calling this a salad doesn't actually do it justice. With a hunk of bread for mopping, it makes a decent light lunch.

For 4

a thick 500g (1lb 2oz) piece of beef fillet, at room temperature
175ml (6fl oz) flavourless vegetable oil (sunflower, groundnut),
   plus a splash extra
salt and pepper
4 tbsp Dijon mustard
1½ tbsp red wine vinegar
2 tsp caster sugar
a splash of hot water
5 tbsp chopped dill
a few handfuls of watercress
extra-virgin olive oil

Preheat the oven to 220°C/425°F/Gas Mark 7. Rub the beef with a splash of oil and season well. Heat an ovenproof frying pan on the hob – without any oil – until it's searing hot. Add the beef and cook for 1½–2 minutes each side and 20 seconds each end. Move it to the oven and cook for 12 minutes, for rare meat. Remove from the pan and put to one side until it has cooled to room temperature.

When the beef is cool, whisk together the Dijon mustard, vinegar and caster sugar until smooth. Vigorously whisk in the vegetable oil, a drop at a time to start with, then in a thin stream, until the sauce is thick. Blitzing it with a hand-held electric blender, if you have one, is the best way to make the sauce emulsify. Finally, whisk in 1 tablespoon hot water and stir in the chopped dill.

Carve the beef into medium slices and arrange them decoratively on a large plate. Splash some of the sauce over the top, then scatter nonchalantly with watercress. Add a few splashes of extra-virgin oil and a bit more salt and pepper. Tip the rest of the sauce into a jug and let people ladle it on at will.

Leeks vinaigrette with tarragon and hazelnuts

There is something magically good about floppily cooked leeks smothered in a gentle mustard dressing. It's a textural as well as flavour thing: silk and satin. The additions of tarragon and hazelnuts are, I think, good ones, but try it once without.

For 4
8 medium leeks, white and palest green only
mustard dressing (page 256)
a handful of tarragon leaves
a handful of chopped chives
a handful of toasted hazelnuts, chopped

Clean the leeks well, examining them carefully at the cut end to make sure they aren't harbouring any grit. Bring a large pan of water to the boil. Throw in the leeks and cook for 8–10 minutes, or until they are silky textured and easily pierced right the way through with the tip of a knife. Particularly large leeks may need a little longer.

Drain the leeks well and arrange them in a serving dish. Splash some mustard dressing over the top – how much is up to you – and leave to cool to room temperature. Scatter the tarragon, chives and hazelnuts over the top.

Winter slaw

A punchy, crunchy mix of midwinter flavours. This is great with cold roast beef or a rare steak.

For 4
1½ tbsp lemon juice
2 heaped tbsp Dijon mustard
6 tbsp extra-virgin olive oil
salt and pepper
2 apples, cored but not peeled
200g (7oz) celeriac, peeled
300g (10½oz) red cabbage
2 handfuls of parsley, chopped
2 handfuls of pecans

In a mixing bowl, whisk together the lemon juice, mustard, oil and some salt and pepper. Cut the apple and celeriac into matchsticks and quickly toss with the dressing to stop them browning. Cut the hard core from the cabbage and discard, then finely shred the leaves and add to the bowl, along with the parsley. Crumble in the pecans and toss everything together until thoroughly mixed and coated.

Duck breast, pear and blue cheese salad

A hefty main-course of a salad this, of the sort you might hope to find in
a roadside café in southwestern France.

For 2
1 tbsp red wine vinegar
½ tsp Dijon mustard
2 tbsp extra-virgin olive oil
salt and pepper
1 duck breast, skin on
2 ripe pears, sliced
2 big handfuls of watercress or mixed baby leaves
1 small round shallot, finely chopped
50–75g (1¾–2¾oz) blue cheese
a handful of toasted hazelnuts

Mix the vinegar and mustard, then beat in the olive oil and some seasoning.
Keep to one side.

Make a crisscross pattern in the duck skin with a sharp knife, without cutting
through to the flesh. Season on both sides. Heat a large frying pan – without
oil – over a medium heat and cook the breast, skin side down, for 8 minutes,
or until the skin is crisp and golden brown and the breast has given up most
of its fat. Tip off all but 1 tablespoon fat. Turn the breast over and cook for
another 3–4 minutes; a big one will need the full 4 minutes. Remove from
the heat and leave in a warm place to rest for 5 minutes. It should be pink
in the middle.

While the duck is resting, halve and core the pears, then slice them
lengthways. Toss with the salad leaves and shallot and most of the dressing.
Divide between two bowls. Scatter over the blue cheese, then slice the duck
breast and arrange it on top. Scatter with the hazelnuts and splash with a bit
more dressing before serving.

Celeriac and beetroot salad

A wonderful combination of earthy sweetness and rooty astringency. This is, I think, properly called Salade Belle Hélène. At least, that's what my mum calls it – and I'm not going to argue with my mum.

For 4

500g (1lb 2oz) beetroot, trimmed of their roots and leaves
500g (1lb 2oz) celeriac
juice of ½ lemon
1 tsp Dijon mustard
1 tsp red wine vinegar
1 quantity mustard dressing (page 256)
a big handful of parsley, roughly chopped
a big handful of chives, roughly chopped

Preheat the oven to 180°C/350°F/Gas Mark 4. Wrap the beetroots individually in foil, put them in a roasting tin and cook in the oven for 1–2 hours, depending on size, until easily pierced to the centre with the tip of a knife; check after 1 hour. Remove from the oven and leave to cool. Peel off the skin – it should slip off with the help of a knife – and cut the beetroot into chunks or slices.

Meanwhile, peel the celeriac and cut it into pieces about 5cm (2in) long and 5mm (¼in) thick. As you cut them, throw them into a bowl of water into which you have squeezed the lemon juice; this will stop them from turning brown.

Bring a saucepan of water to the boil, then drain the celeriac and throw it in. Bring back to the boil and cook for 5 minutes, or until softened. Then drain well and leave to cool.

Whisk the mustard and vinegar into the mustard dressing, then toss with the celeriac and beetroot. Leave everything for a few minutes to get acquainted, then mix in the herbs and serve immediately.

Prawn, chicory and grapefruit salad

This has a slightly retro 1970s feel to it. I think it's probably something to do with the grapefruit: half a grapefruit was considered an exotic restaurant starter back then. Or maybe it's the prawns: prawn cocktail, and all that. Whatever – it's rather refreshing.

For 4

1 grapefruit, yellow or pink
2 heads of white or red chicory (Belgian endive), separated
2 handfuls of watercress
1 tbsp finely chopped shallot or red onion
2 avocados, peeled, stoned and sliced lengthways
2 big handfuls of cooked and peeled cold-water Atlantic prawns
salt and pepper
extra-virgin olive oil

Cut the peel and pith from the grapefruit with a sharp knife, then carefully remove the segments by slicing down either side of the papery membranes. Put the segments in a bowl with the chicory, watercress, shallot or onion, avocado and prawns. Squeeze over any juice from the grapefruit membranes – and tip in any from your chopping board – then season well. Add a glug or two of olive oil and toss lightly together.

Purple sprouting Caesar salad

Sprouting broccoli has a sprightly freshness that so many winter vegetables lack, and I sometimes treat it like asparagus, dipping it into a puddle of hollandaise. This salad, though, plays on its affinity with anchovy and garlic, flavours that feature in Caesar dressing and happen to work particularly well with broccoli, sprouting or otherwise.

For 4
500g (1lb 2oz) purple sprouting broccoli, trimmed
6 canned anchovy fillets in oil
2 garlic cloves, crushed
2 egg yolks
1 tsp Dijon mustard
zest of ½ lemon, plus 2 tbsp juice
salt and black pepper
200ml (7fl oz) mild olive or groundnut oil, plus extra for frying
a big handful of grated Parmesan, plus a few flakes for scattering
2–4 slices of white bread, crusts removed

Separate the broccoli heads from the thickest part of the stalks, and slice the stalks lengthways into halves or quarters to help them cook through. Bring a big pan of salted water to the boil and add the broccoli stalks. Simmer for 3 minutes, then throw in the heads and cook for another 4–5 minutes, or until soft but not disintegrating. Drain in a colander or sieve and run under a cold tap for 30 seconds to stop them cooking. Give them a shake and leave to drain thoroughly.

Mash the anchovies to a paste with the garlic. (I usually do this by roughly chopping them, then smearing everything together on the board using the flat side of a kitchen knife.) Whisk the paste with the egg yolks, mustard and lemon juice, adding a grind or two of black pepper. Next, slowly whisk in the oil, drop by drop at first, until things start to thicken, then in a slow stream. You want to end up with something the consistency of thin mayonnaise. Beat in the grated Parmesan.

Cut the bread into small cubes. Heat a couple of splashes of olive oil in a large frying pan and fry the croûtons until golden brown on all sides.

Toss the broccoli with half the dressing. Arrange on a big plate and scatter the croûtons over the top. Splash with more dressing (you may not need all of it), then sprinkle with some of the grated lemon zest and a handful of shaved Parmesan. Add a good grind of black pepper and dig in.

Roast sweet potato and goat's cheese salad

I'm ashamed to say that for years I'd never cooked a sweet potato, but living in south London there came a point when I could ignore it no longer. I'm still to explore its full potential, but roasted in the oven with some gentle spice, it makes a pretty mean salad.

For 4
a handful of whole blanched almonds
750g (1lb 10oz) sweet potatoes
2 red onions, peeled and cut into eight
2 tsp cumin seed
a pinch of crushed dried chilli flakes
2 garlic cloves, unpeeled
finely grated zest of 1 orange and juice of ½
6 tbsp extra-virgin olive oil
salt and pepper
2 tsp red wine vinegar
4 handfuls of baby spinach leaves
200g (7oz) soft white rindless goat's cheese

Heat a dry frying pan over a medium heat, then throw in the almonds. Cook, stirring occasionally, until tinged with gold.

Preheat the oven to 180°C/350°F/Gas Mark 4. Peel the sweet potatoes and cut them into 2cm (¾in) chunks, then throw them into a roasting tin with the onions, cumin, chilli, garlic and orange zest. Add 4 tablespoons oil, sprinkle with salt and toss everything together until well coated. Put the tin in the oven for 35 minutes, or until the sweet potatoes and onions are soft, turning them over halfway through.

Remove the garlic and squidge the pulp out of the skins into a small bowl. Mash roughly with a fork, then add the orange juice, red wine vinegar, a good pinch of salt and a grind of pepper. Mix well and stir in 2 tablespoons olive oil. Toss the sweet potatoes and onions with the dressing and spinach leaves, then blob the goat's cheese over the top and scatter with the toasted almonds.

I once wrote an article called 'How to Grow a Soup'. It started with instructions for making chicken stock, which the next day morphed into a chicken and vegetable broth, and the day after became a chunky, smoky meal in a bowl, thick with bacon and beans. Soup is such a sustaining thing. Children should be taught how to make it in school.

It is often the answer to what I call my half-hour hunger, the need for something quick and satisfying. The basic formula starts with onion, garlic, celery and carrot, chopped and softened in a pan, along with some bacon and herbs or a bit of spice. From there you can go anywhere. I often just throw in a bit of potato and any other roots that happen to be lying around, then top the whole thing up with stock and leave it to bubble away for 20 minutes. Sometimes I mash it, sometimes I liquidise, sometimes I just leave it as it is.

It may not always be a masterpiece, but it always does the job. And, if nothing else, it's a good way to keep the fridge under control.

French
onion soup

Five-spice
butternut soup

Smoked haddock
and potato soup

Savoy cabbage
and white
bean soup

Parsnip soup
with rosemary

Lentil and
lemon soup

Winter
soup

French onion soup

This is one of those bistro classics that used to be wildly popular but now seems to have slipped off the culinary radar. It's a pity, because when it's good, it's very good. This rendition contains a decent glug of port, which gives it a luxurious richness and depth.

For 4
50g (1¾oz) butter
2 tbsp olive oil
1kg (2lb 4oz) brown onions, peeled and sliced
3 garlic cloves, finely chopped
leaves from 4 sprigs of thyme
2 bay leaves
200ml (7fl oz) ruby port
1.5 litres (2¾ pints) beef stock
salt and pepper
12 thin slices of French bread
100g (3½oz) Gruyère, grated
50g (1¾oz) Parmesan, grated

Heat the butter and oil in a large saucepan and add the onions, garlic, thyme and bay leaves. Stir over a medium heat for 5 minutes, or until the onions start to soften. Reduce the heat a little, cover the pan, and cook for another 35 minutes, or until the onions are properly soft and starting to brown. Give them an occasional stir to stop them burning.

Remove the lid, turn up the heat and cook for another 10 minutes, stirring often, until the onions are sticky and golden brown, again being careful not to let them burn.

Pour in the port, scraping any sweetly caramelised bits from the bottom and sides of the pan. Stir over the heat for 1–2 minutes, or until the booze has pretty much evaporated, then add the stock, turn down the heat and simmer gently for about 20 minutes. Season to taste.

Meanwhile, toast the bread and mix together the two cheeses. Heat the grill to medium. When the soup is done, ladle it into heatproof bowls and drop three slices of bread on top of each one. Scatter some of the cheese generously over the top and place under the grill for 1–2 minutes, or until it is bubbling and gold. Let it cool for a few minutes before you dive in – otherwise you risk straying into burnt tongue territory.

Five-spice butternut soup

I think of this as the 'Cream of Tomato Soup' of the squash world. It has a
similar enveloping sweetness, and also happens to require almost as little
effort as opening a can of Heinz.

For 4

1 medium butternut squash (900g–1kg/2lb–2lb 4oz), peeled, deseeded
  and chopped
4 decent garlic cloves, peeled but whole
2 tsp Chinese five-spice powder, plus a few pinches extra
1 tbsp caster sugar
500ml (18fl oz) chicken stock
50–100ml (2–3½fl oz) double cream
salt and pepper

Put the squash and garlic in a large saucepan with the five-spice powder,
sugar and stock. Season, bring to the boil, then simmer for 20–25 minutes,
or until soft. Pour into a liquidiser or blitz with a hand-held electric blender
until totally smooth, thinning with a splash of water if necessary, then stir in
the cream. Taste and season, then ladle into bowls and sprinkle with a pinch
of five-spice before serving.

Smoked haddock and potato soup

This smoky, silken soup lies somewhere between a New England chowder and a Scottish cullen skink. It's the kind of thing I often find myself craving on a dank winter's day. You might want some crusty bread to go with it.

For 4
600ml (1 pint) whole milk, plus extra if needed
200ml (7fl oz) double cream
1 bay leaf
400g (14oz) undyed smoked haddock fillets
4 tbsp olive oil
6 rashers of smoked streaky bacon, cut into thin strips
1 onion, finely chopped
1 stick celery, finely chopped
2 medium leeks, white and pale green only, sliced thinly
salt and pepper
2 medium potatoes
juice of ½ lemon
a handful of chopped parsley

Put the milk, cream and bay leaf in a saucepan, add the fish and bring everything to a murmuring simmer. Let it bubble gently for 5 minutes, then remove from the heat and leave to stand.

Meanwhile, heat the oil in another, larger saucepan. Throw in the bacon and cook for a couple of minutes, stirring occasionally, until just starting to brown. Stir in the chopped onion, celery and leeks so everything is coated in the fat. Add a couple of good pinches of salt, turn the heat down low, then cover with a lid and cook for 20 minutes, stirring occasionally to stop things sticking. You want the vegetables to be soft and buttery but not brown.

While the other vegetables are cooking, peel the potatoes and cut into slices about twice as thick as a £1 coin. Cut each slice into strips, then across into small cubes. Remove the fish from the pan, keeping the milk and cream, and peel off the skin. Break the flesh into flakes, getting rid of any lingering bones, and keep to one side. Bin the bay leaf.

When the vegetables are soft, add the potatoes and cooking milk from the fish and simmer very gently, without a lid, for 15 minutes, or until the potatoes are soft enough to squidge easily with a fork. Stir in the lemon juice, taste and season. Mash the soup lightly – you can thin it with an extra splash of milk at this stage if you want, though it should be on the thick side – then add the haddock and warm through over a gentle heat. Ladle into bowls and scatter with parsley and a sprinkling of fresh black pepper.

Savoy cabbage and white bean soup

This is a thick and sustaining winter bowlful that straddles the boundary between soup and stew. If you find yourself with kale or cavolo nero rather than cabbage, use them instead. You'll need to strip the leaves from the woody stems, so start with about 350g (12oz).

For 4
2 tbsp olive oil
150g (5½oz) smoked streaky bacon, roughly chopped
1 medium onion, finely chopped
2 celery sticks, finely chopped
2 medium carrots, finely chopped
4 plump garlic cloves, roughly chopped
leaves of 1 sprig of fresh rosemary, finely chopped
2 bay leaves
400g (14oz) can haricot or other white beans, drained and
   rinsed (you need about 250g/9oz drained weight)
1.5 litres (2¾ pints) chicken stock
freshly ground sea salt and black pepper
200g (7oz) Savoy cabbage leaves, roughly sliced
extra-virgin olive oil, for sprinkling
Parmesan, for grating

Heat the oil in a large saucepan and fry the bacon until just golden. Stir in the onion, celery, carrots, garlic and herbs and sweat until soft. Add the drained beans and chicken stock, stir well, then bring to the boil. Turn down the heat and simmer for 25 minutes.

Scoop out and discard the bay leaves, season the soup generously and lightly mash with a potato masher or fork, so that about half the beans are reduced to mush and half remain whole.

Add the cabbage, stir well, then return to the boil and cook for another 7–8 minutes, or until the leaves are soft. Check the seasoning, then ladle into bowls, adding a splash of olive oil and a generous grating of Parmesan before serving.

Parsnip soup with rosemary

Parsnips are fundamentally rather a lumpen vegetable, but I love their curious combination of earthy and sweet. This simple soup turns them into something surprisingly luxurious.

For 4
50g (1¾oz) butter
750g (1lb 10oz) parsnips, peeled and chopped into cubes
2 garlic cloves, peeled, but left whole
1 litre (1¾ pints) chicken stock
300ml (10fl oz) whole milk
salt and pepper
a few rosemary leaves

Melt the butter in a large saucepan, then throw in the chopped parsnips and garlic cloves and season well. Stir over the heat for a couple of minutes until everything is bathed in butter, then add the stock and simmer for 20 minutes, or until the parsnips are soft. Add the milk and heat without boiling, then whizz everything with a hand-held electric blender or in a liquidiser until smooth and thick. Taste and season.

Finely chop the rosemary. Decant the soup into bowls and top each one with a pinch or two of rosemary.

Lentil and lemon soup

I blame hippy cuisine: for a long time, lentils had a reputation as more of a penance than a pleasure. This soup is undeniably wholesome, but the combination of nutty puy lentils with fragrant lemon and herbs makes it anything but hair-shirt.

For 4
2 tbsp olive oil, plus extra for drizzling
1 onion, finely chopped
1 celery stick, finely chopped
1 medium carrot, finely chopped
3 garlic cloves, finely chopped
salt and pepper
200g (7oz) puy lentils
leaves from 2 sprigs of thyme
1 bay leaf
zest and juice of 1 lemon
1.25 litres (2 pints) chicken or vegetable stock
a handful of mint leaves
4 handfuls of baby spinach leaves

Heat the olive oil in big saucepan, then stir in the vegetables and a pinch of salt. Put over a low heat, stir, cover and sweat gently for 10 minutes.

Add the lentils, thyme, bay leaf, lemon juice, zest and stock. Simmer over a gentle heat for 40–45 minutes, or until the lentils are soft. Remove the bay leaf.

Liquidise a third of the soup and add it back into the rest. Taste and season well. Stir in a good handful of mint leaves and spinach and leave to wilt. Serve with olive oil and more mint leaves on top.

I hadn't originally planned a chapter on booze, but I like a drink and it just sort of happened.

There has been a cocktail revolution since I came of age. Most of the 1980s was a festival of bad taste and punning titles. Cocktails tended to be either nasty creamy concoctions with names like Sex on the Beach and The Orgasm, or drinks, such as Long Island Iced Tea, which involved pouring every conceivable spirit into a glass and topping it up with Coke. The bar staff might have been able to throw a bottle in the air and catch it behind their backs – Tom Cruise has a lot to answer for – but most of them didn't know how to mix a good drink.

Sometime in the early 1990s, all that changed. You could suddenly get a proper martini (cold gin in a cold glass) and refined drinks like the Cosmopolitan – citrus vodka, lime juice, triple sec and cranberry – arrived from America. They tasted clean and modern, but with an accompanying sense of ocean-liner chic. A quiet alchemy returned to the other side of the bar.

I should probably warn you that some of the cocktails that follow are rather on the strong side. If you're going to have a drink, I say have a proper one.

A word about booze

The 123

My grandfather loved a party and this was his cocktail of choice. 'Now, Lukey,' he would say with a twinkle in his eye, 'I thought we might have a 123.'

The 123 is a mix of gin and two kinds of vermouth, a wonderfully old-fashioned drink in this age of the very dry and the very sweet. My grandfather learnt it from his father-in-law, who in turn got it from a bartender in Antibes, some time in the 1920s. My dad now makes it on his birthday. It is a cocktail with considerable punch. One is too few, two is just right and three is invariably too many.

By the way, I'm not generally one for favouritism, but if you can get your hands on a bottle of the sweet vermouth called Antica Formula, it knocks spots off all the rest.

For 1
ice cubes
3 tbsp good dry gin
2 tbsp extra dry vermouth
1 tbsp sweet red vermouth
2cm (¾in) strip of lemon peel

Half-fill a tall glass or cocktail shaker with ice cubes. Pour the gin and vermouths over the ice and stir slowly for about 30 seconds. Strain into a small, chilled martini glass. Twist the lemon peel sharply over the glass so the lemon oil from the skin spritzes over the top of the drink. Drop in the peel.

The Cardinal

This is a red kir, made with crème de cassis and chilled Beaujolais or other light red wine instead of the usual white. It's heftier than the white version and, I think, rather more satisfying.

For 1
1 tbsp crème de cassis
125ml (4fl oz) chilled light red wine

Pour the cassis into the bottom of a wine glass. Top up with the chilled red. Drink.

The Negroni

I love the herbal quality of Campari and this uses it in a powerful mix of bitter, sweet and strong. I think it's pretty much a perfect drink.

For 1
ice cubes
2 tbsp good dry gin
2 tbsp Campari
2 tbsp sweet red vermouth
2cm (¾in) strip of orange peel

Half-fill a tall glass or cocktail shaker with ice. Add the gin, Campari and sweet red vermouth and stir together gently for about 30 seconds. Fill a tumbler with more ice cubes and strain in the Negroni. Twist the orange zest over the top and drop it in.

The Spritz

This is the Venetian classic, made with Campari, Aperol or, occasionally, Cynar bitters, topped up with either Prosecco or white wine and soda. I like it best with Campari, but either way, it's a refreshing and sophisticated sharpener.

For 1
1 tbsp Campari
125ml (4fl oz) chilled Prosecco
a slice of orange

Pour the Campari into the bottom of a tumbler or wine glass and top up with the Prosecco. Drop in the slice of orange.

The Hanky Panky

An old-school cocktail, invented in the early 1900s by Ada Coleman, the female head bartender at the Savoy. The first time I tried it – more than a century later, at the basement bar of the splendid Hix restaurant in London's Soho – it instantly became one of my favourite tipples. It's a very grown-up drink: gin and sweet vermouth enlived by the merest splash of Fernet Branca, an almost medicinal brand of Italian herbal bitters.

For 1
ice cubes
3 tbsp good dry gin
3 tbsp sweet vermouth
a dash of Fernet Branca – 1 tsp
2cm (¾in) strip of orange peel

Half-fill a tall glass or cocktail shaker with ice. Add the gin, sweet vermouth and Fernet Branca and stir together gently for 30 seconds. Strain into a cocktail glass. Twist the orange zest over the top and drop it in.

Raspberry and mint caipirinha

Mojito, daiquiri, caipirinha: I find the combination of lime, sugar and booze ludicrously easy to drink. This is a colourful spin on the Brazilian version. You could also make it with vodka or white rum.

For 1
7–8 raspberries or blackberries
1 tbsp light muscovado sugar or light brown sugar
½ lime, cut into four bits
5 torn mint leaves
crushed ice
3 tbsp cachaca

Keep back a couple of the raspberries. Put the rest in a sturdy tumbler with the sugar and lime and pound them with the end of a rolling pin until the juice from the limes and berries has run and is thoroughly mixed with the sugar. Add 3 of the mint leaves and give them a quick bash, then fill the glass with ice. Pour over the cachaca. Stir until the red juices and booze start to mix.

Throw in the remaining raspberries and mint leaf.

This is mostly a gathering together of recipes for things mentioned in a supporting role elsewhere in the book. Some of them, like salsa verde and mayonnaise, are an essential part of what I call the 'dip and lick' style of eating – meat, fish or vegetables, simply served with something good to dunk them in.

I've also, though, thrown in a couple of potato recipes. There are few meals that don't benefit from a bowl of spuds. As a child, I ate so many that I was known as the Potato King.

Bits and pieces

Mayonnaise, aïoli and other good things

Homemade mayonnaise is a quivering pleasure, richer and silkier than most of the stuff you can buy in a jar. It's much easier to make than its reputation might suggest. If the eggs, mustard and oil are all at room temperature and you add the oil slowly, you really shouldn't have a problem. If your eggs are straight out of the fridge, warm the bowl with hot water for a few seconds, then dry it before adding the yolks. The residual heat in the bowl will warm them through.

By the way, I feel a duty to make the following public service announcement: homemade mayonnaise uses raw egg yolks and, though the risks are negligible these days, you should avoid them if you are pregnant, ill, very young or very old.

Makes 1 bowlful
250ml (9fl oz) groundnut or sunflower oil
50ml (2fl oz) extra-virgin olive oil
3 medium egg yolks, at room temperature
2 tsp Dijon mustard
1 tbsp lemon juice, plus a few squeezes extra
salt and pepper
a pinch of sugar

Tip the oils into a jug – you want to be able to pour them easily.

In a mixing bowl, whisk together the egg yolks and mustard for 30 seconds or so until they are well blended. Still whisking constantly, start to add the oil, literally drop by drop at first, until the mixture begins to thicken. When it does, you can start whisking in the oil in a thin, steady stream.

When half the oil has been added, the mayonnaise should be unctuously thick and glossy. Whisk in 1 tablespoon lemon juice, then continue beating in the remaining oil. When it has all been incorporated, season the mayonnaise, adding a pinch of sugar and being generous with the salt. Beat everything in, then taste and whisk in a good extra squeeze of lemon – more if it needs it.

The mayonnaise will keep in the fridge for a couple of days. Cover the surface with clingfilm to stop it forming a skin.

For aïoli
Add 3 crushed garlic cloves to the yolks at the beginning. Be generous with the extra lemon juice at the end.

For lemon mayonnaise
Grate in the zest of 1 lemon. Be generous with the extra lemon juice at the end.

For herb mayonnaise
Make a batch of lemon mayonnaise, then add 1 heaped tablespoon each of finely chopped flat-leaf parsley, basil, chives and tarragon; this is good with cold poached fish or chicken. Or use 3–4 tablespoons of a single herb.

For tartar sauce
Make a batch of mayonnaise, then add 2 tablespoons each of finely chopped shallot, finely chopped flat-leaf parsley and finely chopped tarragon, plus 2–3 tablespoons each of finely chopped gherkins and finely chopped capers (rinse off the salt or squeeze out the vinegar from the capers beforehand). Much will depend on the strength of the gherkins and capers – taste as you go.

Salsa verde

I've included this recipe for the simple and very good reason that it's one of the most deliciously useful sauces there is.

3 big handfuls of flat-leaf parsley
a handful each of basil and mint leaves
5 salted anchovy fillets in olive oil, drained
1 big garlic clove, peeled and crushed
2 tbsp capers (rinse off the salt or squeeze out the vinegar before using)
1 tbsp Dijon mustard
2 tbsp red wine vinegar
125ml (4fl oz) extra-virgin olive oil, maybe a splash more
salt and pepper

Finely chop most of the herbs with the anchovies, garlic and capers. Then roughly chop the remaining herbs – this will give the sauce a bit of texture. Put all the chopped stuff in a bowl with the mustard and vinegar and stir together well, then slowly mix in the olive oil until you have a loose, sauce-like consistency. Precisely what that means is up to you. Season generously.

Mustard dressing

This is my standard dressing, a thick concoction that coats leaves beautifully and even perks up those old-fashioned British lettuces of which there seem to be unaccountably high piles in the supermarkets. It's also rather good poured into the pit of an avocado half and scooped out with teaspoonfuls of the smooth green flesh – one of those simple, sensual pleasures that nobody seems to eat any more.

This quantity is enough for at least a couple of green salads: any extra will keep for a few days in the fridge, though it may need a good whisk every so often to stop it from separating.

2 tbsp Dijon mustard
2 tsp red wine vinegar
2 good pinches of caster sugar
salt and pepper
50ml (2fl oz) extra-virgin olive oil
50ml (2fl oz) flavourless oil (groundnut or sunflower)

Whisk together the mustard, vinegar, sugar, and salt and pepper with 2 teaspoons warm water, until everything is thoroughly combined. Still whisking furiously, gradually add the oil, a few drops at a time to start with, so everything thickens and emulsifies – a bit like a mayonnaise. The faster and more vigorously you can blend the oil with the other ingredients, the longer the dressing will stay emulsified. Using a hand-held electric blender, if you have one, blitzes everything together particularly effectively.

Roast potatoes, big and small

People are very particular about their roast potatoes. Some seem actually to like them soggy. For me, though, they have to be crisp on the outside with a fluffy, almost mash-like middle. This is how I do it.

Eat them as soon as possible after they leave the oven – roast potatoes don't like to be kept waiting.

For 6

2kg (4lb 8oz) medium-sized floury potatoes – preferably King Edwards or
  Maris Pipers
cooking fat: either light olive oil, sunflower, dripping or goose fat
sea salt flakes
a few whole garlic cloves, in their skins
a few sprigs of rosemary or thyme or both

Peel the potatoes and cut them in half lengthways (my preference), or into chunks about 5cm (2in) square — that's half a medium potato, maybe a third of a slightly larger one. Put them in a saucepan of salted boiling water and return to the boil. Once they're bubbling, cook for 7 minutes, then tip into a colander. Give them a good shake for a few seconds, so the outsides go fluffy, and leave them to steam-dry. The drier the outsides, the better. I often leave them for 1 hour. It won't hurt.

Preheat the oven to 200°C/400°F/Gas Mark 6. Pour enough fat into a large roasting tin to cover the bottom, then place in the oven for 10 minutes until it's thoroughly hot. Add the potatoes in a single layer, leaving a bit of space between them. Turn them in the fat, then sprinkle with sea salt flakes. You could also add a few squashed garlic cloves in their skins, plus a few sprigs of rosemary, thyme or both. Cook for 45–55 minutes, turning once, until crisp and golden. Salt and serve.

By the way

If you're cooking these with a roast in a single oven set at a lower temperature, heat the fat in a roasting tin on the hob, rather than the oven. Add the potatoes, turn them in the fat until they start to crisp and brown, then put them in the oven. If they need to crisp more at the end, you can always turn the oven up to 240°C/475°F/Gas Mark 9 for a few minutes, once you've taken out the roast to rest.

A rather nice small version

These have an almost chip-like quality that makes them as good with a steak as with a roast. You'll need fewer potatoes – probably only about 1.25kg (2lb 12oz) for 6 people. They need to be well spread out in the fat, so use two roasting tins if necessary.

Cut the potatoes into small chunks, about 2–3cm (¾–1¼in) square. There's no need to boil them. As with the bigger potatoes, preheat the oven to 200°C/400°F/Gas Mark 6, put in a tray of fat and leave it to get hot. Toss the cubes of potato in the heated fat, adding a sprinkle of salt, plus a few whole garlic cloves and thyme and/or rosemary sprigs as you see fit. Roast for 35–40 minutes, turning halfway through, until crisp and golden brown, with soft insides. Salt well and serve.

Buttery mash

Sometimes basic mashed potatoes is all you want, but this buttery version has a particularly duvet-like comfort. A potato masher will get you only so far when it comes to getting rid of lumps. Putting the cooked potatoes through a potato ricer or old-fashioned vegetable mill (mouli) gives a better texture, and pushing them through a metal sieve is best of all. It takes only a few minutes. Either way, you need to do it while the potatoes are still warm.

For 6
1.5kg (3lb 5oz) King Edward or Maris Piper potatoes, peeled
125ml (4fl oz) whole milk
150g (5½oz) butter
salt and pepper

Cut the potatoes into even slices 1cm (½in) thick. Put them in a pan of salted boiling water, bring back to the boil, and cook for 15 minutes, or until the biggest pieces are soft and falling apart. Drain well in a colander.

Next, either mash them in the pan, put them through the finest holes of a potato ricer or vegetable mill or – my preference – rub them though a metal sieve. This honestly takes only a few minutes.

When the potatoes are mashed, put the purée back into the pan and stir over a low heat for a couple of minutes to dry out if necessary. Add the milk and stir for a couple of minutes more, then stir in the butter until the whole thing is silky and smooth. Season with plenty of salt and pepper and stir in.

Pastry, short and sweet (and savoury)

Both sweet and savoury versions of this pastry have a crumbly, almost flaky texture. The quantity below makes more than enough to line a 23cm (9in) round tart tin.

Both are made in exactly the same way: the sweet pastry just has added sugar and vanilla.

For plain shortcrust
200g (7oz) plain flour
a good pinch of salt
125g (4½oz) cold unsalted butter, cut into cubes
1 medium egg

For sweet shortcrust
200g (7oz) plain flour
a good pinch of salt
125g (4½oz) cold unsalted butter, cut into cubes
1 medium egg
¼ tsp natural vanilla extract
50g (1¾oz) icing sugar

Start by putting the flour and salt in a food processor, using the metal blade, and whizz them together for a few seconds so they're thoroughly mixed (this also does away with the need to sift the flour). Add the cubes of butter and pulse for 5–10 seconds – using half-second bursts – until the mixture looks like coarse breadcrumbs. Don't worry if you can still see the odd tiny fleck of butter, that's fine.

Break the egg into a small bowl with 1 teaspoon cold water. If you're making plain pastry, just lightly beat the egg to break it up. If you're making sweet, whisk in the icing sugar and vanilla as well, until everything's combined.

Add the egg mixture to the food processor and pulse in until the mixture starts to clump together in clods. Stop before it forms a big clod around the spindle.

Tip the dough out onto a work surface and use your hands to gather it together into a coherent mass, squidging in any loose bits of mixture. This takes a matter of a few seconds. The idea is to be as hands-off with the pastry as possible, to stop it becoming tough; you don't want to knead it, just gently press it together. Quickly shape the pastry into a ball, flatten it slightly so you have a disc, then wrap it in clingfilm. Put it in the fridge and chill for at least 1 hour, then roll and bake according to the recipe.

Index

Books are never a solo effort. Though any imperfections are down to me alone, there are people far more gifted than I who have made this one what it is. Thanks to Tara Fisher, Valerie Berry and Wei Tang for the beautiful pictures and styling, and to Emily for teaching me not to double dip; to Lizzy Gray and Helen Hawksfield, my editors at Collins, for asking me to do the book in the first place and shepherding me through the process so kindly, expertly and patiently; to everyone at 'The Sunday Times' for allowing me to indulge my greed on its pages, particularly Tiffanie Darke, the editor of 'Style' magazine, who had enough faith in me to give me the gig, and Kara O'Reilly, who was my editor for the first three years of the column; and to my family, friends and neighbours for putting up with me and providing willing tastebuds.

Finally, thank you to Lucie. I really, truly couldn't have done it without you.